KSRoom
978.1
FIS

ABY-8876
2706113
Y0-AEA-204

OLATHE PUBLIC LIBRARY
OLATHE, KANSAS 66061

JAMES J. FISHER

THE BEST OF
JIM FISHER

EDITED BY ROGER O·CONNOR

Mostly Books
Pittsburg, Kansas
1992

Copyright © 1992 by Roger O'Connor

All rights reserved.
No part of this book may be reproduced or
transmitted in any form or by any means
without permission in writing from the Publisher.

All essays were originally published by the *Kansas City Times*
and the *Kansas City Star*. The editor gratefully acknowledges
the *Kansas City Star* for permission to reprint these essays.

Library of Congress Cataloging-in-Publication Data

Fisher, James, 1937-
   The Best of Jim Fisher / James J. Fisher : edited by Roger O'Connor.-- Pittsburg, Kan. : Mostly Books, 1992
   154 p. : 26 x 18 cm.

   ISBN 1-882355-00-8
   ISBN 1-882355-01-6 (pbk.)
   1. Kansas--History. 2. Missouri--History 3. West (U.S.) -- History. I. O'Connor, Roger, 1941-   II. Title.
   978.1

Additional copies of this book are available from:
Mostly Books
111 East Sixth Street
Pittsburg, KS 66762

Printed in the United States of America

To my mother, Lucile Jaquith Fisher, and

_____

to my father, Paul W. Fisher--

Writer, Editor, Friend.

TIGHTWAD, Mo.--and Bland, Spickard, Rascal Flats....

Yes, these are real towns--off the beaten path, to be sure, but this is Jim Fisher's country, and he's been going through it like a garage sale for some fifteen years now, delighting the readers of his thrice-weekly "Midlands" columns in the *Kansas City Star* and *Times* with people and places and things they would not have otherwise known.

It is a country all his own, wherein he takes an old story or a chance discovery and lets it become a vehicle for introspection. Through his eyes, a collection of hammers illuminates our past, a small country store is the same social institution that it was 150 years ago, and we share his delight at some stroke of fortune, wince at the stark reality of frontier medicine, and snort at the practical joke, which--then as now--is neither practical nor jocular.

Jim Fisher does not "report" on the Midlands--"news" is left to others. But he does, I think, bring us closer together as neighbors, and as human beings. There are so many concentric circles in our lives: we are Kansans, Big Red supporters, Elks, golfers, etc. *ad nauseam*--but each link we discover helps us locate ourselves. Jim Fisher links all of the above, and he links us to ourselves as people, and we are better for the wisdom of his shrewd eye in finding this commonality.

Jim Fisher does not live in the past, despite its preponderance in my selection, but he does often tie the past to the present--perhaps to show us how little we have really changed, how very **human** we are. And the people whom he finds, with his uncanny human pheremone, are wonderful: some are famous, and some are not, but the fact that the world did not beat a path to their doors makes them no less important in the eyes--or the columns--of Jim Fisher.

I wonder what a new copy editor would say upon receiving his first Jim Fisher column? After all, does any other newspaperman in America consistently (and gleefully) use the word "goofy"? And what about sentences without verbs, or single adjectives standing sentinel and alone? It took me quite a while to realize that Jim Fisher is not (like most writers) concerned with how words **look** on paper, but how he can represent the way speech **sounds** on paper. He reproduces conversation, as well as the weights and flavors and nuances of words. For besides a nose for a good story, Jim Fisher has an ear for the rhythms of speech and vernacular, and always--always--a penchant for the straight-faced aside or the epigrammatic remark, which he uses, unobtrusively, as his punctuation.

And there is humor in Jim Fisher's words--above all, he is **fun**. Not only the stories that he fishes for us, but his artistry in relating them attest to what is, I think, a storyteller of such great ability that the reader doesn't realize the "how" of his being entertained. All of us like a good story, but Jim Fisher can take the kernel of a tale, add a word here, elicit a remark there, and turn it into something like the three-nail horseshoe story, where all the reader can say upon completion is -- "Neat!" If Jim Fisher were a mapmaker, he'd put in rocks and trees.

While Jim Fisher is fun, he is also funny--and he is not selfish with this gift. He is a master of understatement who knows the value of incongruity-- the real basis of all humor.

But the most remarkable quality of all, to me, is Jim Fisher's love of people. Perhaps this is in my imagination only, but I prefer to see in his Midlands an affirmation of the "human-ness" of us all, be it a Civil War soldier or an artist or a storekeeper of 60 years' duration or a farmer of 60 years' tenacity. The lives of each of us--all of us--touch, and if there is a common denominator in Jim Fisher's writing it is the fact that we all have a deep-seated fealty to values and responses that have been part of us for hundreds of years. Without sounding "goofy," it is difficult to articulate emotional aspects of the human condition; yet in a small quiet way it is our responsiveness to the things that have gone before that makes us what we are, and we can imagine that, one hundred years ago, there were other men that considered war, and fear, and beauty, and the joy of watching a horse run or a child play, and we can say silently "Yes, I understand. I feel that way, too."

Thanks, Jim.

RO'C
Pittsburg, Kansas
September 1992

April 12, 1992

You Could Identify Them by the Nails in Their Horseshoes

TOPEKA -- Over in Kansas City there's a tempest in a teapot over the name of the thoroughfare that runs along the Kansas-Missouri border, namely State Line Road.

Some have suggested renaming the road, saying the name is archaic, divisive and hardly fitting to a great metropolitan area.

Others--with blood in their eyes--have rushed to State Line's defense. It's the state line, they say, so call it that and forget this political correctness tripe.

That faction will doubtless prevail. Place names, unlike those of human beings (re: the Missouri political candidate who recently changed his moniker to include ''Bullet Train'') are hard to change. There's custom and tradition involved.

Anyway, think of the mess it would be to change all the stationery and business forms already out there.

Still, if things ever get to a point where a name change is in the offing, here's a suggestion:

''Three-Nail Road.''

No, you're right, that name isn't exactly inspiring. It's not one that would lead people to forget bi-state rivalries, start looking at Greater Kansas City as one big city rather than a bunch of separate communities, or bring sweetness and light to the various cranks on both sides.

Three-Nail Road. You may not realize it, but that's a name with everything--history, anger, bloodshed, midnight chases on horseback, thievery, plunder, even murder.

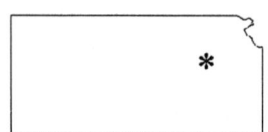

Three-Nail Road comes to us courtesy of Albert Robinson Greene, who was 70 when he wrote his recollections for the Kansas State Historical Society in 1912.

Greene was a former member of the Ninth Kansas Cavalry, stationed in Kansas City, Westport and Jackson County during the Civil War. His service came as each side made cross-border forays that invariably resulted in the loss of life, property and innocence.

The combatants--the bushwhackers on the rebel side and the Jayhawkers who supported the Union cause--viewed the state line as a very real thing. It wasn't just a dirt road, running north and south.

On the Missouri side were the occupying Union forces, surrounded by a seething mass of citizens sympathetic to the bushwhackers.

On the Kansas side, Union forces were doing essentially the same thing-- acting as military policemen. In the Sunflower State, the job was to keep wild-eyed Kansans from invading Missouri to rape, pillage and kill. Which they still managed to do with almost monotonous regularity.

Back then, the state line was truly a line in the sand.

Greene was well into his remembrances when he dropped one of those little nuggets that fascinate people who like history.

Since Green was a member of a troop that chased bushwhackers all over the place, a question for may always has been this: in those days, before soldiers ran around in T-72 tanks on one side and M1-A1 tanks on the other, how could you tell who was who?

Simple, wrote Green. Horseshoes.

The bushwhackers thereabouts, namely William Clarke Quantrill and his band of cutthroats, were on short rations. Not just victuals, but also farrier supplies.

In 1863, having a well-shod horse was as important as a full tank of fuel on a modern-day Bradley fighting vehicle.

No fuel, no Bradley. No horseshoe, no horse.

In especially short supply, it seems, were horseshoe nails. So the bushwhackers made do. Instead of using four nails on each side of the shoe as was the ordinary way of shoeing, they used three.

Thus a hoof print of a bushwhacker's mount would show six nails instead of eight. For the Ninth Kansas Cavalry troopers, the bushwhackers might as well have left calling cards.

Greene wrote that scouting missions by the Ninth always looked for the telltale three-nail sign. And nowhere were those signs more avidly searched for than along the Kansas- Missouri state line.

Three-nail tracks heading west? That meant somebody in Kansas was in for a very bad time.

The same coming east? That meant the bushwhackers had done their job and were coming home, across the state line, across what was essentially Three-Nail Road.

Which, if you say it often enough, has a ring to it. Admittedly, not a great ring. But there's a little something there. . . .

March 1, 1983

Clutter Let Him Clean Up

NEVADA, Mo. -- When C. Robert Quitno bought the W.F. Norman Corp. here in 1978, he was buying space--specifically 50,000 square feet.

The red-brick structure northeast of the square was maybe a little run down at the heels from time. But it was perfect for what Mr. Quitno, 54, wanted, which was to become a wood-burning-stove mogul.

Mr. Quitno--his name is Norwegian--had been in farm implements, in both the production and dealership end, but he wanted his own business. Stoves seemed right for the times. He had a prototype that he thought would go like gang busters.

And, shortly after moving into the plant, Mr. Quitno produced a few of the stoves.

But there was a problem back then--the plant's clutter. Scattered almost everywhere were old metal dies weighing up to a ton each and a bunch of ancient metal-stamping machines operated not by hydraulic fluid, compressed air or computers but by--would you believe--belt drives and ropes. Ropes!

What is this? Mr. Quitno politely asked of Franklin Norman, the grandson of the founder of the company, the man who had sold him the business and who was staying on during the transition. Well, said the gracious Mr. Norman, now in his 70s, this is what we used to make pressed metal ceilings 40 or 50 years ago. Oh, you've seen them in old stores, Mr. Norman said, sometimes painted other colors. they were *the* ceiling back then. Uniquely American, too.

Of course, that was long past, since gypsum and plaster and acoustical tiles

had taken over modern ceilings. But about 124 dies, each detailing a different design, from Greek to Colonial, Rococo to Empire, Gothic to Oriental --enough so Mr. Quitno later could reprint the 1909 Norman catalog almost word for word, picture for picture -- were still in the factory. So were a good number of the original plaster of Paris die molds. And the old rope drop hammers that were ideal to pound out the ornate ceiling panels were in place.

There hadn't been any real need to get rid of the stuff, mused Mr. Norman, because the plant was plenty big and the 1978 Norman product line -- metal stall showers, temporary grave markers, funeral home "no parking" signs and metal planter boxes--didn't require much space.

Mr. Quitno, although the owner of the old business for a short time, could understand just by looking around. The firm really didn't look that much different from the way it must have at its founding in 1898. Roll-top and stand-up desks were in the offices along with ancient chairs, and even glazed tile fireplaces were in the two executive offices. It was as if time -- including World War II scrap drives, the love of American business for modern fixtures, even fire and natural disaster -- had passed the business by. The phrase Mr. Quitno thought of was "time warp."

Mr. Norman inquired: did Mr. Quitno want him to get bids from scrap dealers to come in and haul out all the old stuff? Mr. Quitno, who had about a million-watt light bulb going on over his head, demurred and got on the telephone to the Gilbert-Robinson restaurant people in Kansas City.

Mr. Quitno knew one thing--the nostalgia craze was taking off. From his phone call, Mr. Quitno found out that to put a pressed metal ceiling in a Country Club Plaza restaurant, Gilbert-Robinson had to tear down an old building with such a ceiling, remove the ceiling and then reinstall it. That was no cheap matter. Sadly, such ceilings just weren't available anymore, he was told, except from a New York supplier who had only a limited number of designs.

Mr. Quitno threw some samples of the ceiling panels in his car and drove to Kansas City, where he met with Gilbert-Robinson people and some others. They told Mr. Quitno bluntly that he had the next-best thing to a license to print money.

"Every year has been better than before," Mr. Quitno said last week.

"Business is absolutely booming. We've done a room in Mary Pickford's home, Pickfair. We've sold to every state and Australia. Europe looks good. We may do a room in the Smithsonian. We sell to architects, restaurants, do-it-yourselfers. No, I haven't changed anything. When buyers come to the factory, they step back into yesterday. I like that."

Mr. Quitno doesn't think the success of the company is transitory. The demand is too steady. People want the fancy ceilings. But what about the stoves he was going to make?

"Oh, anybody can make those," Mr. Quitno said with a smile.

April 1, 1986

Cemetery Story Has a Sequel

BROWNING, Mo. -- It's just a little thing, said Robert Shanks. Still, he said, people might like to know.

When Mr. Shanks was referring to was a story that appeared in this space last fall. It was about the Gooch cemetery here, a true Missouri cemetery where the emotions that the state's politics have engendered over the years have been laid out, literally, for all eternity.

In the Gooch cemetery, Democrats are buried on the west side. The Republicans are buried on the east. A path goes through the middle of the cemetery, separating the two factions.

"People around here always thought bad blood was why the cemetery was laid that way," said Mr. Shanks, a spry man of 79 and a Gooch on his mother's side.

" 'Course that wasn't it at all. It was just politics."

But the Gooch cemetery, unique as it is, wasn't what brought Mr. Shanks to the hill where the cemetery sits. He was looking west.

"Now there -- near that old persimmon tree. That's where the Gooch slave quarters were," he said. "Years ago you could see the old log foundations. But they're gone. Farming, you know.

"But right down here is what I want you to see. See that pond? And where the ditch runs into it? Well, that's where it was. Right there."

And all of a sudden, in his own mind, Mr. Shanks was back to 1915 or 1916, remembering those days when he and his twin brother, Richard, would wend their way to school across Gooch land.

They were 8 years old or thereabouts. To them places where dead people resided were, well, scary. So the boys would walk west of the Gooch cemetery and east of where the pond is now. Back then there was a fenced-in area -- another cemetery.

"That was where the Gooch Negroes were buried," Mr. Shanks said.

Every so often the two boys would screw up their courage and go into the slave cemetery, marveling at the names on the stones -- Big Annie and Little Jake, Cripple Ike and Old Granny. No last names. And on especially brave days they'd put their ears to the ground on the graves, listening for the Negro spirituals that they thought were supposed to emanate from the graves. They heard nothing.

Back then, the twins had never even seen a black man. But the boys' grandfather, Hezekiah Shanks, a Kentuckian who'd settled here, had pounded in their heads that men all bled the same, no matter what color. And reinforcement for that came when the twins were 9 years old and Henry Shanks came up from Kentucky to visit Grandpa Shanks.

Henry Shanks was black, a former slave of Grandpa Shanks back in Kentucky and freed here after the Civil War.

There was a whole separate story about Henry Shanks -- a man who married, had three children and then lost them when their master sold them. Grandpa Shanks mortgaged his farm and gave Henry Shanks the money to buy them back. And Henry Shanks had repaid the debt.

"Henry was old, like Grandpa," Mr. Shanks said. "When he came, well, I think they slept in the same bed."

Jim Crow was the custom then. But it was ignored, at least in the Shanks household. Just two old friends with their common afflictions -- their age, their bladders and their bittersweet memories.

"I never forgot those two," Mr. Shanks said. "And for years, when I farmed this land, I always plowed around the old slave cemetery real careful. You know, respect.

"I quit farming in '52. After that they put in the pond. I don't think they knew. So the cemetery is gone. Which is a shame."

As Mr. Shanks said, it's just a little thing. But, he said, people ought to know.

August 25, 1983

History Should Jog Its Memory

JUNCTION CITY, Kan. -- Probably not a dozen living Kansans have ever heard of Thomas Allen Cullinan, the tough Irishman who ruled this town as marshal for the last 30 years of the 19th century.

But consider:

· Although Irish, he became the master of an English vessel, no small feat considering the antipathy of the British at that time for their kin across the Irish Sea.

· Coming to America he was a Great Lakes sailor, river pilot, lumberjack, gold miner, sutler and Civil War scout.

· In 1860, accompanied by two other men, he descended the first 250 miles of the Colorado River toward California before being captured by Ute Indians. If not for the Utes, the name Cullinan probably would be in the history books instead of that of John Wesley Powell, the first man to trace the river to the sea. Mr. Powell made his journey in 1869.

Mr. Cullinan's pre-Junction City accomplishments would fade, however, during his 30 years of service to this U.S. Army post town. From 1871 to 1900, with time out for a couple of years as chief enforcement officer for the Metropolitan Street Railway in Kansas City, Tom Cullinan ran this town with an iron hand.

Civil libertarians would've hated Mr. Cullinan. Writing of the town marshal, one contemporary said:

"In the '70s and the '80s, when the town was more turbulent than of late, he enforced the law in his own way with the hearty approval of the entire population. That is, if Tom deemed it proper, he could take a man before police court or lock him up, and it was

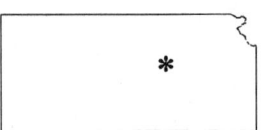

all right.

"If he deemed it proper to administer the law by walloping the earth with a sinner, that too was deemed all right."

Mr. Cullinan was very good with his fists. There were countless stories of roughneck Army recruits, loose on their first pass and full of liquor, going back to Fort Riley in ambulances after tangling with Mr. Cullinan. George Martin, later secretary of the Kansas Historical Society and, for a time, mayor of Junction City, recalled instances in which Mr. Cullinan was actually afraid of the gun he carried, knowing that once it was loosed from its holster, all sorts of nasty things could happen.

And, of course, Mr. Cullinan's reluctance to use a gun ultimately meant that he would be forgotten by history. He was not Wyatt Earp, Bat Masterson or Wild Bill Hickok, quick with a pistol or shotgun, men to be found -- at least in the mind's eye of the dime novelists and the Hollywood directors-- dealing cards at a poker table and then rising when trouble reared its head and going into the street for the classic confrontation with a doomed miscreant.

The disappearance into the mists of history in the case of Mr. Cullinan wasn't uncommon. West of here at Abilene, one of the greatest of the cattle towns, there's a Tom Smith Street, a Tom Smith Stadium and a 2-ton granite block marking his grave at the Abilene cemetery. Tom Smith?

Mr. Smith, like Mr. Cullinan, cleaned up his town with his fists in 1870, resigned to become a deputy U.S. marshal and, unfortunately, was beheaded by an ax-wielding man he was trying to arrest near Chapman Creek. The people of Abilene didn't forget, but history, again in the form of the dime novel, did. It ignored Mr. Smith but almost beatified Hickok, the latter a man whom Abilene residents recalled as one whose "bearing and bravery were of a low type."

Nobody ever said that of Tom Cullinan. In 1884 an amateur prizefighter came to Junction City from Clay Center expressly to test Mr. Cullinan's mettle. The man raised a ruckus in the afternoon. Mr. Cullinan told him to get out of town. The man, a red-haired fellow, didn't, and raised another row.

Finally, at the Pacific House, the marshal had had enough.

"Now, I will take you in," Mr. Cullinan told the man. The man slapped Mr. Cullinan in the mouth, uttering some foolishness about Mr. Cullinan's manhood.

That was a mistake. In seconds Mr. Cullinan had "beat the man to tatters," especially on the head. A few hours later the man was on an eastbound train, never to return, a mass of dried and clotted blood from the top of his head to his waist.

That was Tom Cullinan. Nothing fancy, but he got the job done. And in 1904 he died in bed.

December 22, 1989

And a Grand Time Was Had by All

(KANSAS CITY, Mo.)--The papers say office Christmas parties are definitely out of favor, a result of deep-pockets litigation and what's essentially a revival of the old temperance movement.

Which is OK. Times change.

Even so, some folks look back on those long-ago parties, remembering some good times, some bad times, and wondering how on earth they survived it all.

Now, instead of office parties, some companies, including this one, have started giving gift certificates allowing the bearer 20 bucks of groceries at any of a number of supermarkets. That's good corporate thinking. Lawsuits don't usually flow from an employee buying tortilla chips, a carrot cake and a half a gallon of low-fat milk.

Some of those old parties, though, were classics. Like one in the early 1960s given by this newspaper. It's worth remembering for a moment since this is the last Christmas ever that there'll be a *Kansas City Times*. Next year this journal will have a different name.

That particular Christmas party, held at a tony Johnson County country club, had its moments. And remembering them, one almost has to concede that today's grocery certificates may be as valuable to the maintenance of domestic bliss as preventing any court case involving drunken driving on the way home.

It was more than just a party. There was a whale of a fistfight between some of the wives, numerous cases of unconsciousness and three, count 'em, three divorces.

As C.W. Gusewelle, columnist for *The Kansas City Star* has pointed out, *The Times* crew in those days was a raffish lot.

There was a police reporter who had the habit of changing clothes and bathing but every three months; a courthouse reporter who was soon to disappear into thin air; and, of course, the elderly copy editor whose wife used to sit in the parking lot during his 8-hour shift, convinced she would catch him consorting with painted ladies, despite the near-terminal condition of his health.

The company then allowed something like $6 a head for dinner and drinks *and* a band. The organizer of this party was a Runyonesque character whose wife once found him in the most compromising position a man can be found in by his wife. Yet somehow, the organizer, now dead, managed to convince his wife she hadn't seen what she most certainly had seen.

As usual, there had been early partying at various places before the formal Christmas gathering. Things got off to an inauspicious start when one of the big bosses at the paper, a man who favored large, expensive cigars, announced to a group of reporters that he had just spent $43,000 redecorating the kitchen of his Mission Hills home.

This statement was not well received since reporters then mainly lived in cheap apartments and thought $95 a week was big money. But they kept their mouths shut. The man with the cigar could fire them on the spot. And in the 1960s, there was no appeal.

And that was the last thing they wanted, being young and full of beans, convinced that getting paid for chasing fire engines, covering gangland murders, being in on the aftermath of bank robberies was all some wonderful mistake anyway.

Unlike some of the new journalists, seriousness was not in their makeup. Newspapering was fun.

But the $43,000 redecorated kitchen was soon forgotten. One reporter passed out in mid-sentence, his face landing in his plate. And there he remained.

Another slid under a table. An obituary writer vanished, soon to be found in the back room, insensible, a pint bottle in hand.

And even those events soon were eclipsed by a clatter in the women's restroom. Some wives had gone there "to powder their noses."

One had found tissue paper missing in her stall and called out for another wife to throw her a box of Kleenex from the vanity.

Which the other wife did, throwing the box, still clad in its heavy metal dispenser, over the door and whacking the supplicant in the head, leaving a gash and causing considerable bleeding.

That's when the fistfight started.

Things went downhill from there. To say there was considerable tension would be to understate the case. Hardly anyone danced.

And it was apparently at this point that three couples began heated discussions over journalistic behavior that would result, in the coming months, in their names being printed in the "Divorces Granted" column of the paper.

Still, months later, most of the unwounded, undivorced and unembarrassed would look back and remember that winter night with a certain fondness.

"Great party," they'd say.

November 20, 1989

Channel Meeting Local Need

ST. JOHN, Kan. -- Somehow it seems simpler out here. Even something like cable television.

Take what was S.J.M. Cable. The initials stood for St. John and Macksville, the latter being 12 miles over to the west. The company, until recently, was owned by its founders and builders, George and David Cutright--father and son, television repairman and music teacher.

Naturally, since this is central Kansas, S.J.M.'s headquarters wasn't one of those fancy buildings, the kind cable companies in bigger places have.

Half of the elder Cutright's cluttered garage did just fine, thank you, for engineering space and a studio.

And because the cable business is what it is today with conglomerates gobbling up small-town companies, the Cutrights had offers to buy.

Which is what they wanted to do-- George to finally retire, David to continue his varied vocations of piano tuning, television production and computer programming.

Eventually they sold to an outfit called Multivision. But first they did some dickering.

"We've always had Channel 9 for local origination," says David. "Want ads, death notices, recipes, birthdays--stuff like that. Community service."

So when the offers came--and there were several--the Cutrights put one proviso on any negotiations.

They'd keep running Channel 9.

"Without that, well, we just didn't talk to them," says David. "We thought the channel was important to the towns."

Multivision accepted the proviso. And Channel 9 has continued. Not too many towns of comparable size can refer to what folks here call "our television station."

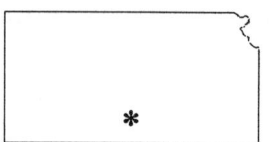

That means that from dawn to midnight announcements, obituaries, upcoming events, lost pets, local news, etc., appear on the screen. They're all typed into a device and continually updated by David's daughter, Amy, 15.

At noon viewers get live television with what's called the St. John Journal, an eclectic talk show with local businessmen and businesswomen appearing as "anchors."

The Journal does interviews with anybody and everybody. Likely as not, that's a neighbor on the screen. And if there's government problem, they'll get a local official in. It can be lively, says David, especially when all 12 seats in the studio are full.

Plus Channel 9 does City Council meetings, church services and election results. All live, too.

"We keep it pretty simple," says David. "No real bright lighting, no makeup."

Not surprisingly, the Cutrights have kept up with the flap in Kansas City where the Ku Klux Klan wants to be on the community access channel. David makes the point that Channel 9 here is "local origination," not "local access." There's a big difference, he says.

One other thing. Channel 9 does all the St. John Tigers home basketball games.

"We tried doing football for a while but they have this old press box that literally sways in the wind," says David. "And the lights are fine for the crowd but not for television. Anyway, Dad was freezing to death up there."

And how is "our station" being received?

Just fine, David says, with a lot of comments from older people confined to their homes. He adds:

"One of the most popular shows is when I just go out on a nice day and walk around town with the camcorder running.

"You know, just a show telling what the town looks like now. Older folks really like that.

"People say it's nice to see, even if it is just pictures with no narration. They tell us that more than anything it brings back lots of memories."

February 26, 1992

Candidate's Big Barbecue Cost Him the Election

BUNCETON, Mo. -- Politics is a primary topic these days, so it might do well to recall a political campaign that foundered, but not on the current shoals of sex, character, or dubious financial dealings.

No, this one went belly up over a barbecue. And it happened in Missouri in 1924.

That year the Democratic candidate for governor was Arthur Nelson, a physician who'd never practiced and who instead had become a banker and landowner. His showplace farm near here was known as "Eastwood."

Nelson's Republican opponent was Sam Baker, a former school administrator.

Thanks to William B. Claycomb of Sedalia, writing in the *Missouri Historical Review*, we have a picture of that campaign, the barbecue, and a lot of Missouri voters who apparently got madder than hornets.

Politics was more leisurely 68 years ago. Both Nelson and Baker won their August primaries easily. Campaigning in those days started in September.

The main issue, then like now, was the economy. The boom of the 1920s had ignored most Missouri farmers. Commodity prices were low, rural banks were failing, and farm-to-market roads were terrible.

Nelson looked like a shoo-in, what with this state's Democratic heritage and his kinship to two of the state's most revered political families--the Sappingtons and the Marmadukes.

There was a flip side. The Republicans, right off the bat, claimed Nelson was a member of the Ku Klux Klan, a

charge the candidate denied, although he admitted he had attended a Klan rally as a spectator. Republicans pooh-poohed his claim of being a "dirt farmer," since Eastwood was 3,600 acres of manicured fields and pastures. Nelson, said the GOP, was "a farmer who never farmed, a banker who never banked, a doctor who never doctored, and a Kluxer who never Kluxed."

In turn, Nelson's forces charged that the current governor, Republican Arthur M. Hyde, had a working still in the governor's mansion and that the state's chief executive was little better than a bootlegger.

And we worry about negative campaigning today?

Nelson and his lieutenants figures to start his campaign off Sept. 15, 1924, with a massive barbecue at Eastwood. The guest speaker would be John W. Davis, the Democratic standard bearer who'd meet Calvin Coolidge in the Nov. 4 election for president.

Eastwood ordered 10 tons of beef and mutton, 14,000 watermelons and other victuals. Naturally, everybody was invited. Everybody.

After scattered showers the night before, Sept. 15 dawned clear and dry, as people started pouring into southern Cooper County from across the state.

How many? Claycomb estimates 60,000 people. Fields containing 260 acres became parking lots.

So many came that a problem arose: By midafternoon, the food was gone-- the beef, the mutton, even every last one of the watermelons. There were grumbles.

Still, it looked like a successful gathering. At 2 p.m. Nelson spoke. An hour later Davis gave his speech, finishing at 3:40 p.m.

Five minutes later it began to sprinkle. Soon buckets of rain were coming down.

As Claycomb recounts, people scrambled for their cars but only a third escaped before the fields became bogs.

Local roads were no better. For miles in every direction, cars ended up in ditches or mired up to their hubs in mud.

Those who came on trains or were stuck in the parking lots were stranded. At least 20,000 of those, Claycomb says, had had nothing to eat. They took shelter on the porches of Eastwood or under some tents.

And there they stayed the night. In fact, some didn't get home for days-- hungry, muddy, tired and furious.

When the governor's returns were counted 50 days later, Baker had 49.4 percent; Nelson 48.9; and two minor candidates 1.7 percent. Coolidge, incidentally, won Missouri easily with 54 percent of the vote.

Claycomb notes that fewer than 3,000 votes separated Nelson and Baker. Surely there were that many disgruntled barbecue guests.

"Up to a few years ago there were still people in this country who'd been at the barbecue," recalls a Cooper County resident. "And who were still mad."

December 29, 1989

A Glimpse Backward at Glory

PITTSBURG, Kan. -- Remember movies like "Sergeant York"? Or "All Quiet on the Western Front"? Surely "Platoon"?

Well, the trailers for a movie called "Glory" are out, teasing television viewers with bits of what's essentially a slam-bang war movie. But one with meaning, usually a sure-fire recipe for box-office receipts.

"Glory" may be a 1990 blockbuster--a Civil War epic of the black soldiers of the 54th Massachusetts Infantry, freedmen, field hands, former slaves and fugitives who had to fight to get into the war and then were decimated during their glorious charge against Confederate lines at Fort Wagner, S.C., in July 1863. Thus the movie's name.

The New York Times splashed the film all over its Arts and Leisure section last spring when it was still in production. The reviewers are raving.

And starting next week--the movie opens nationally Jan. 19--one can expect to see the stars on the morning television shows, making "Glory" not a word, but a title.

Big stars, too. Morgan Freeman who plays the hard-bitten sergeant; Denzel Washington, the troublemaker; Matthew Broderick, the young commanding officer.

And big bucks. The film reportedly cost $18 million. Include the promotion costs, and it all adds up to very serious money.

All of which brings a bemused smile to the face of a slender man who daily walks across the campus of Pittsburg State University here, enters old Russ Hall and climbs the stairs to his cluttered office.

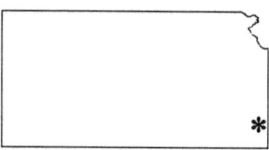

Dudley Taylor Cornish, professor emeritus of American history, knows all about the 54th Massachusetts and Fort Wagner. Heck, he wrote *the* book.

No, not the screenplay. The book--a volume titled *The Sable Arm*, called "one of the 100 best books ever written on the Civil War," "a classic," "a standard," and "timeless."

Quite simply, if you want to understand the black soldier in the Civil War, read Cornish. Forget for a moment the actors in the movie and look at the background, the nuts and bolts. Cornish laid the groundwork.

The title comes from the Old Testament eloquence of Frederick Douglass, who knew early on that the conflict wouldn't be a couple of skirmishes outside Washington and then a quick surrender by Richmond. It would be total war, thundered Douglass, and the North would need "the sable arm" of black Americans to "strike down slavery, the source and center of this gigantic rebellion."

Which, as Cornish chronicled, the North eventually did, raising 165 "colored" regiments--roughly 175,000 men or 12 percent of the Union forces, a fact that for years was omitted in the history books. A third of the black men died in a service that treated many of them like dogs, paid them less, and offered summary execution or a return to slavery if they were captured.

Still, as Cornish has written, black men flocked to regiments such as the 54th Massachusetts, the 30th U.S., the 1st and 2nd Kansas Colored. And their guidons snapped at parade with battle streamers--Port Hudson, Milliken's Bend, Poison Springs, Fort Pillow, Honey Hill, Petersburg.

The genesis of *The Sable Arm* was simple. As an officer candidate in World War II, Cornish had been inducted along with a black man he remembers only as "Eustace." The two were much alike--young, eager, willing to serve. But once at a post for basic training, Eustace told Cornish that "I am going to be in a different part of the Army." Cornish was puzzled. But not for long. The United States Army, in 1942, was Jim Crow.

Cornish, now 74, never forgot Eustace. And after the war he studied history and asked himself what was this "different part of the Army."

The answers, ignored for so long, were everywhere--in official records, historical societies, diaries, newspapers. Between 1867 and 1888 three histories about black Civil War soldiers (all wanting) were written. And after that, silence.

The Sable Arm was published in 1956. In a sense, it opened the floodgates. A bookshelf that would have contained only Cornish's book 33 years ago now would groan from the weight of the published works on the black military experience from Crispus Attucks to Vietnam. Quite simply, a revolution in what's called historiography occurred. No small event in a profession that moves slowly at best.

And Cornish was in the vanguard.

Now comes "Glory," a movie which actor Freeman has described as "the kind of picture that gives legitimacy to the history of people of color, and tells us who we are."

Cornish can't wait to see the movie. But he does have one fear.

"I just don't want people to forget the other 164 regiments," he says.

January 8, 1992

Holiday Gunplay Could Have Ended Two Lives

GREENVILLE, Mo.-- It was a matter of some delicacy.

A young man had been shot in the lung and hovered near death.

The shooter was a member of a rival faction.

Family members of the victim were not happy; in their vocabulary, in fact, was the word vendetta, and they were known to take umbrage at any "family" offense, whether real or imagined.

In that vein, some years earlier, the same family had remonstrated with another man, shooting him in the forehead, face, and chest because they suspected him of an unrelated slight against the clan. That victim, not surprisingly, expired from the family's attention to him with a Navy Colt.

So, back to present, the predicament of the lung-shot victim and the guy who shot him was a dicey matter.

Enter Terry Stephenson, who must have been some kind of negotiator. The man had a silver tongue.

In fact, Stephenson, if still alive, probably would be a natural to mediate the differences between the Israelis and the Arabs; placate the various factions in Southeast Asia; soothe the increasingly fractious members of the new Commonwealth of Independent States; conduct a sit-down with mob families now exterminating each other back east; and even bring calm waters to the various Democrats seeking the party's presidential nomination.

Why? Well, all Stephenson had to deal with was Jesse and Frank James, two men with blood in their eyes.

What had happened was this:

On Jan. 3, 1882, James A. Rhodus, known as "Uncle Jimmy," gave a combined Christmas-New Year's

party. Such bashes were a little different then, running two and three days, since guests came a long way in their wagons and buckboards.

Uncle Jimmy lived outside Greenville, a place that's no longer on the map since it doesn't exist anymore. Greenville was roughly four miles east of Kearney.

One of those attending the party was John Thomas Samuel, 20, maternal half-brother to Jesse and Frank.

Samuel was a young buck, said to be full of vinegar. He'd been way too young for the Civil War and all its attendant excitement. But he held a lot of the old prejudices prevalent in this part of Missouri.

Naturally, the one group Samuel loathed was Republicans.

Uncle Jimmy, unfortunately, happened to be of that political persuasion.

Young Samuel had been drinking and became obnoxious. Words were exchanged. Samuel was ejected from the premises.

At that particular point, Samuel showed his maturity. He started throwing rocks at the house.

By and by, Uncle Jimmy appeared on the porch and told Samuel to cease and desist. Samuel didn't. Guns were drawn. Uncle Jimmy, an old codger of 54, was faster (or Samuel was drunker) and shot the youth in the right lung.

The first reports in the *Liberty Advance* stated the wound was "mortal." Not so.

Walter Plourd, a retired railroad watchman and former mayor of Missouri City, Mo., whose detective work uncovered the all-but-unknown Rhodus-Samuel affair, tracked the recovery of the boy through issue after issue of the Liberty papers. The notices say Rhodus remained at home. Plourd, 64, whose avocation since retirement has been the James boys, figures Rhodus was waiting for the hammer to drop.

"In those days you didn't cross the Jameses," says Plourd. "Uncle Jimmy was an ex-Union soldier. That was one strike.

"Strike two was him being a Republican.

"And the final count against him was that he'd shot one of the Jameses' kin. You didn't do that."

Thus, says Plourd, the negotiating skills of Terry Stephenson must have been considerable. Eventually, after all the palavering by Stephenson, there was a big meeting of the Jameses at the Shoal Creek Church south of here, and Uncle Jimmy's fate was decided.

He would live. The consensus was that Samuel had precipitated what had happened. In short, the idiot got what he deserved.

With that, Uncle Jimmy breathed easier and lived to be 76.

Jesse lived only another three months before being assassinated by Bob Ford in St. Joseph.

Frank ended up in a Wild West show and never served a day in jail.

And Johnny Samuel? He lived until 1932, dying--where else--out in California.

"The legend is that he became a pretty nice fellow after he recovered," says Plourd. "But then I guess getting shot would have a sobering effect on a person, wouldn't it?"

April 25, 1981

He Opened the Night to Baseball

INDEPENDENCE, Kan.-- On Wednesday afternoon, 87-year-old Elva Losey excused herself from guests in the living room of her home at 800 E. Maple St., walked to the porch where some other visitors had gathered and sat down.

"I want to tell the story," she said firmly.

There was silence. "The story" is a tale told often among the Losey clan about the patriarch of the family, Leslie E. Losey. Over the years the story has assumed qualities of a legend. But it's true. The commissioner of baseball and the Baseball Hall of Fame in Cooperstown, N.Y., confirm its essential facts.

"It was 1929 and Leslie was at the University of Wisconsin taking some courses and this electric salesman talked about lights at baseball games," Mrs. Losey said.

"Well, Leslie talked to Charles Kerr, the mayor here, and Marvin Turby, a jeweler, and a man named Ray K. Hart. They decided to put lights at the Riverside Park for baseball for the 1930 season. The electric salesman even came down here to help."

The superintendent of schools and the high school principal, Mrs. Losey recalled, thought Losey--then the physical education director for the Independence schools--was "crazy."

"Well, Leslie waited for those two to go off for a convention," she said. "Then he got signed letters from school board members that they approved. Then they put the lights up on wooden poles."

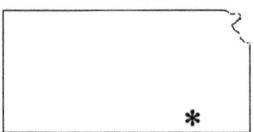

On April 28, 1930, the first night game in organized professional baseball was played here in Independence. The Muskogee Chiefs beat the Independence Producers 13-3.

"Of course when the superintendent got back, he was mad and I think he would have fired Leslie," Mrs. Losey continued. "But Leslie has the letters from the board. So the superintendent let it go but he never gave him or the others credit. But Leslie didn't care. We all knew. The people here knew."

So did Commissioner of Baseball Bowie Kuhn. Last Jan. 1, on Losey's

94th birthday, Kuhn wrote him recognizing his achievement and noting that night games during the World Series now were seen by 80 million people.

"It made him so proud," Mrs. Losey said. "He knew the game was on record back at the Hall of Fame, but the letter was personal and it meant so much."

Mrs. Losey paused.

"This is helping me," she said. "I'm remembering good times, not what's just happened."

Remembering helped everybody. Just an hour earlier, they had buried Leslie E. Losey in Mount Hope Cemetery, dead of bone cancer after months of pain.

After the burial, relatives returned to the house. At first there was little talk. But recollections of Losey, a short, bandy-legged man known as "Paw-Paw" and "Old Bull" to his grandchildren, eased the whispers.

"When I was playing football at KU I remember his bicep was as big as mine and he was past 80 then," said Robert Hammond of Denver, a grandson. "I remember when I was a little kid and he'd lift me on his back when we were fishing and carry me across a river to a sandbar. He was always a superman to me. He never seemed old."

Losey was born in Clay County, Kan., the son of a bronc-buster. He was an all-state basketball player at Emporia State despite being only 5 feet 7 inches tall. In 1913, he came here, to a town without a physical education program for its schools. Within a year, Losey had 2,500 students running, tumbling, doing gymnastics, playing tennis, and in their spare time, clearing the land for Riverside Park. His was the first formal physical education program in the state and was widely copied.

"Erecting the lights obviously seems like the spectacular thing in his life," said the Rev. Paul Peters, a son-in-law from Kunkletown, Pa. "But I think we remember him also for other things--working with disabled and handicapped children long before it was popular.

"He designed the (Losey) gymnasium to include a corrective section for such children. He said physical education was the equal of athletic achievement. Athletic team members always took physical education."

Losey's daughter, Dorothy Peters, recalled a polio victim who had difficulty walking.

"Dad worked to help him develop his upper body and taught him to walk on his hands," she said. "I can remember the boy on the top floor of the high school and then walking down all three floors to the street on his hands. And I remember the big grin he had afterward. Maybe it was a small one, but it was his victory. And it was Dad's too."

March 28, 1986

Wars and Rumors of Wars

MONROE CITY, Mo. -- The papers the last few days have been full of war stories -- from Libya and Central America.

But the reports have been so sketchy that one network commentator use the phrase "the fog of war" to describe events. And that was probably stretching things.

Wars used to be simpler. Take the battle of Monroe City here 125 years ago this coming July. Everybody knew what was going on because most everybody was involved-- either as a participant or a spectator.

Now it's Harpoon missiles and A-7 fighter bombers. And nobody remembers Gen. Thomas A. Harris, commander here of the Confederate forces who that day were trying to whup up on some Yankee blue-bellies. Or what Gen. Harris said that day-- unique for any military commander.

What happened was this:

Union spies had reported there was a bunch of "secesh" hereabouts. Five hundred Illinois troops came to punish them. The Unionists got off the train here on July 8, 1861, marched south to Florida, Mo., and promptly got themselves surrounded by southern sympathizers who were as thick as horse flies.

The federals then marched back to Monroe City and holed up in the local seminary. They got surrounded again. There was sniping back and forth with nobody really getting hurt.

Meanwhile, the country was filling up with people who'd come to see the "war." One writer recalled:

"The greatest excitement arose in

the surrounding country and news that 500 Yankees were 'treed up' in a building in Monroe City spread like wildfire. Messengers, like Paul Revere, went galloping over the country rousing farmers who armed themselves and came to participate in the battle."

The commander of this bunch, which numbered about 1,000 men, was Gen. Harris, a former Missouri legislator known for his "bombastic speech-making and who on every possible occasion and pretext would mount a box and harangue his soldiers."

Or anybody else who was in earshot. Gen. Harris was still a politician.

Still, he managed to deploy his men, ordered up a cannon that had been hidden in a haystack, and started his bombardment.

One problem. He had a 9-pound cannon, but 6-pound cannonballs -- which sort of rattled around inside the gun. It was said the safest place within the range of the cannon when it was fired was directly in front of it. For instance, one ball was fired, landed 30 feet from the muzzle, made an abrupt right turn and then smashed to flinders a Confederate blacksmith shop a quarter of a mile away. Of 25 cannonballs fired, only three hit the seminary.

Naturally, spectators showed up -- about 1,200 of them -- and more than a few of them were drunk. Gen. Harris, like any politician, decided the time was ripe for a speech. His message was unique in military history.

He announced that even though he had the federals outnumbered 2-1, casualties would be high with any sort of frontal attack. Blood would be spilled.

So he suggested everybody just go home.

Of course nobody listened. Their blood was up.

But the point was moot. Gen. Harris had taken so much time speechifying that he'd forgotten to tear up the Hannibal and St. Joe railroad tracks. And guess who arrived about then?

Why, more Union troops. Ones with cannon and ammunition that fit. They opened fire and Gen. Harris and his troops skedaddled, some taking refuge among the rapidly departing spectators, others wildly riding away into the countryside.

The battle of Monroe City was over, consigned to being no more than a footnote in history.

Albeit a simpler one.

August 14, 1991

A Carnival Man Remembers Folks at Home

LEBANON, Kan. -- When news came last month that a fellow named Milton A. Srader had left Smith County a million bucks in his will, folks here scratched their heads.

Milt Srader? Who was he?

Here and there was a spark of recognition. Didn't some Sraders farm south of here a long time ago?

Most people, however, drew a blank, understandable since Milt was pushing 98 when he died in Wichita in 1989. Most of his peers had been dead for years.

And Milt had made tracks out of here as a youth, opting for a life of calliopes and cotton candy, canvas tents and games of chance.

Milt was a carnival operator from the 1920s until the 1950s, bringer of dreams and magic to a thousand small towns. He was the big, raw-boned fellow counting the crowd as it streamed in the gate. He was the purveyor of things most people had never seen--freak shows, Ferris wheels, giant teddy bears, strong men, sword swallowers and stalls selling corn dogs and funnel cakes.

When Milt and his carnival came to town--any town--time was suspended. Wondrously, one end of town would light up for a night or two. And beneath that illumination would be born memories, especially among children, that would grow and still be vivid decades later.

Photographs of a young Milt show a firm jaw and penetrating eyes. In his later years, with a short beard, he resembled the late film director John Huston. His most striking feature was his huge hands, probably needed more than once to knock some sense into a

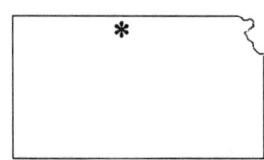

roustabout or rambunctious customer.

Milt smoked cigars. He was known to take a drink. And maybe more than one, too. He was a plunger, willing to bet his carnival--and save it from ruin--on a hand of cards.

He married Mattie Page Srader. They had a daughter, Patricia, who was the apple of Milt's eye until she died unexpectedly in 1968 at age 45. Mattie died in 1980. Milt spent his last years living as a virtual recluse just off Wichita's downtown area. The last couple of years were spent in a rest home.

And there it was that Jim Bush, a lawyer from Smith Center, and Bill Martin, an official of Smith Center State Bank & Trust Co., met Milt.

Milt knew his time was coming. He knew the bank because he'd been with it for years. He was not a poor man, having invested in farmland near Lebanon, adding on to the old home place until he owned more than a section of land.

His real wealth, however, was in certificates of deposit. He had bundles of those, most with a value of $20,000. Each.

A will, written before Mattie died, left most of the estate to her relatives and friends, some of whom Milt didn't even know. Mattie, to use a phrase, was a dominant woman.

But Mattie was dead. Milt wanted to do things his way. For once.

"What he kept coming back to was a time in Oregon when his carnival got stuck," Bush said. "They were set up but it just kept raining and raining. So they were shut down. No money coming in.

"Somehow people in Smith County heard about the pickle Milt was in. They sent packages and food and whatever they could to help. And remember, this was in the '30s when folks back here weren't in real good shape either."

Martin said Milt never forgot that kindness. He wanted to do something for his home county.

So a new will was drawn.

Essentially, the income from Milt's estate was divided--half, or roughly $35,000 annually to Smith County, and half to Ralph Sooter, 84, of Wichita, who cared for Milt in his last years. When Sooter, who knew Milt in the old days, dies, all the income will go to the county for recreational, educational and health related projects chosen by what's called the Srader Foundation.

When Milt died, Feb. 13, 1989, two distant relatives attended the funeral and burial in Phillipsburg, Kan. The will was contested by 27 distant relatives. A Sedgwick County court rejected that suit in July, and the relatives have until Thursday to appeal, something Bush doubts they will do.

"We waited until the suit was settled to announce it to the county," Bush said. "No use getting people's hopes up."

And the reaction?

Milt would be pleased.

April 1, 1982

Scandals Gave Paper Its Flavor

LAMAR, Mo. -- Doug Davis, the publisher of the *Lamar Democrat*, has been taking some kidding around the square here. Since the paper ended 78 years of daily publication and became a weekly earlier this month, folks have been asking if the *Democrat* is going to start writing the news like old Arthur Aull and his daughter used to.

Mr. Davis, a genial Alabama native who owns 15 percent of the *Democrat*, kids right back: "I couldn't afford to have three lawyers full time out at the counter if I did."

But Mr. Davis has been thinking. Maybe, he says, we'll take out the names in the stories and run one a week sort of to give people a taste of how things used to be. Mr. Davis is still toying with the idea. If he does run the stories, he'll be the one to copy them down and set them in type, just to make sure no name is left in inadvertently. For example, here is a 1945 Aull story:

There will be a session of circuit court here in Lamar tomorrow before Judge Brown concerning Miss Blank. She has been stirring around among the boys and has gotten a case of syphilis.

Mr. Aull, who was the editor from 1900 until his death in 1948, and his daughter, the late Madeline Aull Van Hafften, didn't use the word Blank. They used real names in a time when libel laws were looser. And even using Blank doesn't really harm the flavor of the Aull stories. Take this one about a drunk being arrested:

George Blank was arrested in Lamar Tuesday on a charge of drunk driving. George comes to town occasionally. He is very likely to get to driving the

car when he is very drunk. Thus far they haven't hung on him and taken him to the penitentiary. He really doesn't do too much but just get drunk.

"You couldn't write that way today," Mr. Davis says. "The lawyers would be all over you. Invasion of privacy, libel, defamation of character, you name it. But in those days, things were different."

William Bray, executive director of the Missouri Press Association in Columbia, agrees. The laws have changed, he says, and Mr. Aull, who gained a national reputation from his belief in "telling everything," and like-minded Missouri editors like Charles "Polecat" Blanton of the *Sikeston Standard*, who did the same, would be frustrated today--and probably in court much of the time.

"I really don't think people would want to see that kind of detailed stuff in the paper now even if you could print it," says Mr. Davis, recalling that the Aulls printed every allegation in divorce suits, gave graphic details about final illnesses of the deceased ("She had all her female organs removed and then died after suffering a nervous collapse") and even reported who was committed to what state insane asylum.

The Aulls' telling all led *Harper's* magazine to once label the *Democrat* "the brightest star in American journalism." In its heyday, the paper had subscribers in 50 states who avidly awaited the latest scandal in Lamar.

Mr. Davis also was acutely aware of the historical implications of changing the *Democrat* from a daily to a weekly. It had been Mr. Aull who changed the paper from a weekly to a daily in 1904. It was a gut-wrenching decision, Mr. Davis says, one he wrestled with for months. But competing shoppers, newsprint costs, postage and other expenses made the decision inevitable.

"I've had a couple of cancellations," he says. "But we've picked up new readers who say they like the weekly format better. And I know we'll do a better job."

Mr. Davis says he has been trying to emulate one of the most important facets of the Aull legacy ever since coming here a year ago.

If you look closely at the old files, he says, you'll find one thing. The Aulls wrote about people. And readers of any newspaper have an insatiable curiosity about their neighbors. Sure, people will read a story about a new device fitted over a cow's eyes to make her eat less, but what they are really interested in is what people in Lamar are doing.

"You don't have to say who got rejected by the Army because he had a hernia or who's had a brain stroke," he says. "But you do have to tell people what other people are doing."

The thing is, Mr. Davis says, these days you just have to be a little more circumspect.

October 18, 1991

Historians Read Between Lines of Old Ledgers

FORT SCOTT, Kan. --The Daughters of the American Revolution, the National Park Service and the Kansas State Historical Society will gather at 1 p.m. today at the National Historic Site here.

There'll be music, speeches, a short lecture, refreshments. Plus conversation, smiles, even a concluding trumpet fanfare.

And the object of the reception?

Two old, dusty account books, one dated 1844-45, the other 1851-52, found earlier this year in a closet.

The ledgers once belonged to H.T. Wilson, civilian sutler (storekeeper) when Fort Scott was a frontier Army post.

They are a very big deal. Through them, suppositions can be erased or added to, conjectures pushed aside or confirmed, theories either embraced or rejected.

"They tell how this post worked," says Arnold Schofield, the site historian. "We had some records from here and there. But day to day, week to week? The nitty gritty? For us these books equal the Rosetta stone."

The account books were filled by Wilson or his clerks. They're plain-looking volumes with entries such as James Brown buying bed ticking for 25 cents, Dr. J. Walker purchasing five cakes of shaving soap for 50 cents, a Lt. Berry being charged a dollar for a pair of suspenders.

But there's more. The book also records what Wilson himself was buying--lumber, cattle, cases of "segars."

In the last few months, the contents of the books have been entered into a computer. The printout of those old pages is more than 1,000 pages long.

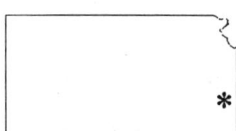

And, from the preliminary study, some rather odd things have emerged.

· Wilson was renting slaves from owners and using them as clerks. Not field hands, not laborers. Clerks.

· The garrison, which history tells us was out in the boondocks, was remarkably well-read. Wilson routinely stocked East Coast newspapers.

· Women were here. Sales of brocades and notions were brisk, indicating that not everybody wore buckskins and calico.

• Wilson was a wholesaler especially to the Chouteau family's Indian trading post east of here. Records of that post have been scant to non-existent. Not now.

"Wilson was big-time," Schofield says. "We thought this was sort of a Mom-and-Pop post. This was a Wal-Mart."

Alan Chilton, museum curator for the National Historic Site, who has been working on the ledgers with volunteers Ora Stuart and Teresa Lowen, says the computer is the key. Chilton says:

"It can tell us what diets were like at certain times of the year; how fishing was in the local rivers through the purchase of fishhooks; what the Indians in the area were buying and selling; even which soldiers were drinking too much."

Wilson himself is a whole other story. But the saga of the ledgers getting from then to now is no mystery.

Apparently the old sutler, who became one of Fort Scott's richest men, parceled his ledgers to three daughters as mementos of his younger days.

His middle daughter, Elizabeth Wilson Goodlander, donated her two ledgers (the others have disappeared) to the Molly Foster Berry chapter of the Daughters of the American Revolution here when she joined in 1911. The books were accepted and placed in a closet in the DAR hall, where they were forgotten.

Last summer Mary Ann French, regent of the chapter, found them. She called Stephen Miller, National Historic Site superintendent. Were he and his staff interested?

Were they? Does the sun come up in the morning?

Discussions were held, and eventually copies were made. Today the DAR chapter will present the original ledgers as a loan to the site until the year 2000, at which time a permanent disposition of the ledgers will be made.

Schofield contends the ledgers will be invaluable to understanding what really happened here a century and a half ago.

A footnote: during the copying of the books, the copier began to rumble and groan. A service technician was called. After four hours he found the problem--sand in the machine's innards.

"Wilson blotted his writing," Chilton says. "Blotting paper then had a high concentration of sand in it to dry the ink.

"Imagine, 140-plus years and that sand jams our copier."

August 21, 1987

Old Drum Could be Trusted

WARRENSBURG, Mo. --The bronze statue of the old hound is hard to miss.

It sits on the sloping lawn of the Johnson County Courthouse here, eternally alert, forever poised in frozen anticipation. Is there a scent of a raccoon in the breeze? Or a coyote off to the south in the woodlands where the dog once ran?

The statue is that of Old Drum, a dog made famous by George Graham Vest, a Kentuckian whose first case as a lawyer in Missouri ended in his client's being lynched. Thankfully, things improved after that.

Vest, an eloquent attorney, was a short, thickset man with an unruly thatch of red hair; one who served his adopted state as a U.S. senator for 24 years. But whose immortality as a Missourian came not in the hallowed chambers of the Senate. His fame came here with an oration about an ordinary but beloved dog.

The case is pertinent today. It dealt with trust--trust in the basic goodness of man's best friend.

Trust. A word you don't hear much these days. Maybe with good reason. We don't seem to be able to trust the president. Or his minions. Or various preachers. Even the Marines seem suspect.

You can't trust the airlines to get you there on time. Drive on a freeway, especially in California in 1987, and there's an off chance you may get shot at.

Trust. You have to be a magician to open an aspirin bottle lest the tablets be laced with cyanide. Or look at a milk carton--there you'll see the ultimate betrayal of trust.

And now the pit bull. The pictures, the stories, the brutal videotape of an animal control officer being attacked by a pit bull in Los Angeles--and the dog not letting go.

And yet with all the pictures, all the stories, there's something else, something we don't talk about.

How many people with a dog bigger than a poodle haven't wondered a little? A twinge here, a doubt there. Look at your dog. He's got teeth.

Can you trust them? And if you can't trust your dog, who can you trust?

That brings up Warrensburg, where some folks in 1956 did a sensible thing. They put up a statue to Old Drum.

The statue sort of puts things in perspective. Dogs are dogs. Pit bulls are aberrations, a product of the times, no different than some of the people who come off the mean streets of 1980s America.

Old Drum was a fine Missouri hound owned by a farmer named Charlie Burden. In 1869, Old Drum was shot dead by a neighbor, Leonidas Hornsby, for supposedly killing a sheep. Burden sued for damages--the loss of his hound.

Burden's attorney was--who else-- George Graham Vest, who said in his closing statement:

"Gentlemen of the jury, the best friend a man has in this world may turn against him and become his enemy. His son or daughter that he has reared with loving care may prove ungrateful. . . .A man's reputation may be sacrificed in a moment of ill-considered action. The people who. . .do us honor. . .may be the first to throw the stone of malice when failure settles its cloud upon our heads.

"The one absolutely unselfish friend that man can have in this selfish world, the one that never deserts him, the one what never proves ungrateful or treacherous, is his dog.

"Gentlemen of the jury, a man's dog stands by him in prosperity and in poverty, in health and sickness. He will sleep on the cold ground where the wintry winds blow and the snow drives fiercely, if only he may be near his master's side. He will kiss the hand that has no food to offer. He will guard the sleep of his pauper master as if he were a prince.

"When all friends desert, he remains. He is as constant in his love as the sun in its journey through the heavens. If fortune drives the master forth an outcast. . .the dog asks no higher privelege. . .than to guard against danger.

"And when the last scene comes and death takes the master and the body is laid in the cold ground, there by his graveside will the noble dog be found, his head between his paws, his eyes sad but open in alert watchfulness, faithful and true even to death."

Corny? Well, maybe a little by today's standards. But Vest won his case. He defined what 99 percent of all dogs are.

Burden got $50.

And Old Drum, quite properly, got his statue.

December 15, 1989

Could This Really be Kansas?

WICHITA -- A hundred or so years ago there was a saloon here called "Rowdy Joe's."

Naturally, the owner was named Joe, remembered later as a short, stocky man who'd as soon deck an obnoxious customer as look at him.

And if that didn't do the job, Joe would shoot the patron dead. "He acted as his own police force," was the way one writer put it.

And if that wasn't enough, Joe had a wife, known as "Rowdy Kate." By all accounts, Kate was a looker, although that has to be taken with a grain of salt. (A contemporary of Kate's was Belle Starr of Georgia City, Mo., and parts west, whose pulchritude also was marveled at. Yet photographic plates show her as quite possibly the ugliest woman ever born.)

Kate was a piece of work. Folks in Wichita said she could drink more than Joe (which apparently was considerable) and was quicker with a six-shooter. She'd fatally ventilated five men. Two of her victims were husbands, indicating Kate wasn't real big on divorce courts when there was a simpler and quicker way.

But apparently, Joe and Kate had a blissful marriage. Leastways until Joe got to arguing with one of his competitors over the cosmic question of which way the Arkansas River ran. Joe said it ran one way; the competitor said another.

Joe drew his gun and quicker than a New York minute he didn't have that particular competition anymore.

All of which says something about Kansas, a state that only three years ago came into the 20th century in regard to liquor laws. Up till then, people regarded Kansas as, well, backward. Which it was, having adopted repressive liquor laws starting in the 1880s and only slowly liberalizing them over the next 100 years.

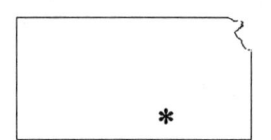

But go back. Maybe there was a reason for everything.

Such as Pawnee, Kan., which had 12 dwellings in it, three of which were saloons--a ratio any drunk would love.

Or Wichita, which had an emporium that sold whiskey, wine, groceries, boots and stoves, all under one roof.

Chanute had 13 saloons, Newton 27 and Topeka, where the sober-minded legislators gathered, more than 100.

So for those who venture into the new, mixed-drink saloons in the big city counties, they should note the ferns, brass railings and polished bars are but modern aberrations, unrecognizable as the progeny of a now-past Kansas landmark.

"In your typical Kansas saloon," wrote one chronicler of the institution, "the only things shiny were the spittoon and the top of the bartender's head."

Those saloons stank--of tobacco, whiskey, beer, spoiled food, tracked-in manure, kerosene, even sizzling spit on hot stoves, left by chewers with lousy aim.

And there were no apologies. That would come years later when bar owners, pressured by the temperance forces, tried to clean up their act.

Apologies? Try defiance, as in this flier distributed in 1872 near what is now Scandia, Kan.:

Republican Valley Saloon
Geo. Morningstar & Sons, Prop.

This notorious establishment takes pleasure in notifying the public generally that it is fully prepared (having on hand a large stock for the trade) to supply at exorbitant rates by the pint, half pint, and drink, to be drunk on the premises or off the premises, by man, woman, or child, preacher, lawyer or doctor, black-leg or bummer, the most diabolical rotgut whiskey ever vended to the public.

Special mixtures provided for church members, put in small bottles, labeled medicine, and deposited for the accommodation 10 steps from the southwestern corner of the saloon.

Candidates for office supplied at wholesale rates.

Beastly drunkenness insured in three drinks. Family ruin in six months. Free fights are an attractive feature of this institution.

In fact we are prepared to sink the morality of the whole neighborhood in a few gulps.

Now that was a saloon.

Of Hume, Zonker and Zig

HUME, Mo. -- Interested in how Hume got its name? You won't believe it.

It seems that back in 1880, Hume was called Howard. It was a nice little town, but folks weren't really satisfied with the name.

Which wasn't all that strange. Howard was a new town in Bates County, not far from the Kansas line. And it was a lot easier to change the name of a new town than an old one. Not that many plats and deeds or other bureaucratic junk had piled up.

Anyway, there was another Howard, over in Elk County, Kan. Now Kansas being Kansas, not a free-and-easy state like Missouri, people out there had to get their potables from afar. Like from a distillery in Kentucky. Somebody in Howard, Kan., with a powerful thirst, ordered three barrels of good whiskey from the Hume Distilling Co. in Louisville, Ky.

Guess where the whiskey ended up? Right. Howard, Mo.

Well, three barrels of sippin' whiskey landing on your doorstep must mean there is a natural order to things. And the citizens of Howard, Mo., then in the midst of a town name-change discussion took the whiskey as a sign. They needed a shorter name, one that wouldn't get confused with any other. Especially if they were ordering whiskey from Kentucky. So they changed the town name to Hume. And most likely drank the whiskey.

Sound a little farfetched? It's true. It's right there in the Robert Ramsay place-name collection at the State Historical Society of Missouri in Columbia. The Ramsay file is 60,000 short stories, all about how places in Missouri got their names.

Take Zonker, Mo., an extinct town in Douglas County. No, it wasn't a creation of the Doonesbury comic strip. Zonker, Mo., was named for a local family named Zonker.

'Course nobody, leastways back in the 19th century, would have thought Zonker funny since there was no such cartoon character then. The same for Zig, an Adair County town, named for a settler, Harrison Ziegler.

You see, the post office used to be the big cheese in naming towns. The officials wanted short or catchy names, ones that wouldn't get mixed up. "Peculiar," was the way one government employee put it. Thus Peculiar, Mo.

But even the post office had its limits. In 1895, Raymond P. Lynch, a man who ran a small post office in Texas County, submitted the name "Odd" to Washington. The mail being the mail, he didn't hear back for two years. So it was Odd, Mo., until 1897 when the post office said Odd was too odd and had him change it to Bucyrus.

Another short name was Ink, allegedly chosen when an ink bottle spilled during the town's debate about what to call the place. That was one story. The other is that George Shedd, the postmaster, got out his third-grade speller and submitted every three-letter word he could find to Washington. Ink came back as the government's choice.

And the government was fallible, too. Joe Gill, who lived down in Dent County before the Civil War, ran the post office at a place named Winston. When the war came, folks cleared out. And when the fighting stopped, Daviess County had the Winston name for a post office there.

Mr. Gill thought about it and decided on calling his post office "Mark Twain" to honor an up-and-coming author he admired. OK, said the post office, which immediately dropped the Christian name and misspelled the surname.

Welcome to Twane, Mo., which, regrettably, no longer exists.

April 8, 1990

Gift to Children Brings Immortality to Produce Farmer

EMPORIA, Kan. -- With the exception of the most misanthropic, most of us dream of some sort of fame. Even for only 15 minutes.

But immortality? Or better said, to be remembered for more than a year or so?

That's harder and a task usually left to a stonecutter. He'll incise a name and some words onto a granite marker, then set it among hundreds of others in a cemetery. The stone will be something people see but rarely read in a place they visit but rarely linger.

But imagine this. Birth in 1853. Death 70 years later. And almost 70 years after that children still shout and laugh nearby. Horses graze. On quiet days, deer wander by. Your stone is carefully tended.

And more. Scores of people are dedicated to keeping your memory alive. Your name is familiar, one people still speak, one that appears on highway signs. It even shows up now and then in the local newspaper.

And still more. Grown men and women fondly recall times they spent not far from your grave. Of games and fishing, of camping and horseback riding.

Now there's a sort of immortality.

Ah, a cynic would say, such a thing would happen only if you died wealthy, if you left huge endowments, or provided money for monster buildings. One would have to be a mover and a shaker.

But an old black man who died alone in a shack? One whose life work was selling vegetables and fruits from the back of a horse-drawn wagon?

His name was E.J. "Jones" Alexander and the memory of him is, for some, even more vivid than that of William Allen White, the famous editor most associated with this east central Kansas city.

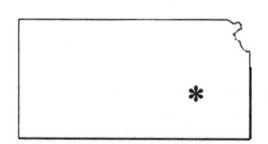

"I remember him," said John Walls, 75, who was 7 years old in 1922, the year before Jones died. Walls lived in the black community in east Emporia.

"I was just a little kid and people have told me since that he had a chant to attract customers. That he had white horses pulling the wagon. I don't remember that. But I do remember a man with a beard who came by every couple of days.

He would go over in the west side and sell to the white folks. Then he would come through our part of town and give what he had left to folks. That's what I remember."

Not surprisingly there's a big park here named for White, whose fame was national and international. But Jones' legacy, called Camp Alexander and used also for nature studies, family reunions, Scout gatherings and a host of other activities, is bigger.

The park is nice, but Camp Alexander, well, it's wonderful, now grown to a 75-acre tract near the Neosho River.

Jones bought his first nine acres in 1886. It was rough land, probably a parcel no one else wanted. A bachelor, he worked hard. Eventually he added 30 more acres.

It was said he had been born a slave in North Carolina. That he had his master's name. That he was far older than he looked, and that he had seen hard times.

Jones himself was silent about his past. People would try to draw him out and he'd invariably clam up. He concentrated on his produce.

He had a touch. From his bottomland gardens came succulent apples, firm, tasty potatoes, peaches that took your breath away. And three times a week he would make the three-mile trip to Emporia. And on his way back, like a 1920s Pied Piper, he would throw apples to the children who followed him or take a sack of fruit to some poor soul who was having it tough.

It was not an easy time to be black. Not even in Kansas. The Klan was resurgent. Walls can remember cross burnings and white robed men in downtown Emporia.

Jones went about his business, his route, his selling.

But in 1922, Jones did an odd thing. He had a will written. Back then, most people died intestate. Not Jones. His will was very specific.

He set aside one acre for not only his grave but for any other person too poor to afford a plot. He made some provisions for his neighbors. And then he left the remainder of his land to all the children of Emporia, Lyons County and the State of Kansas.

It would have been easy then to have written racial restrictions into the will. But not Jones. He knew children don't hate. They have to learn that from adults.

James Putnam, a lawyer here, said the will was unusual not only in its major bequest but also because it was written at all. Most people back then let the probate courts sort things out.

For 16 years, from 1923 to 1939, nothing was done about Jones' will. But then Putnam found it in the courthouse and went out to look at the old place. The fences were down, neighbors' cattle grazed the land, the shack was falling down.

Putnam went back to the courthouse. And the court said there would be a camp for youth.

Which is what happened. Since 1939, with time out for the war, Camp Alexander has been building, bit by bit, year by year, open to all even before the term "civil rights" became familiar.

And more amazingly, over the years hundreds of citizens, black and white, have worked on the camp, providing free labor, building shelter houses, mowing the grass, bringing in horses for kids to ride, hay for the horses to eat.

Black people have always been on the board of directors. Celebrities such as Wilt Chamberlain and Bob Boozer and Gale Sayers have come down to dedicate this or that.

Walls is the current chairman of the board. Clair Garrison is the man who makes things work. He is maintenance vice chairman, meaning he's the chief cook, bottle washer and number cruncher. He said the camp runs on $13,000 a year, half from the United Way, half from private donations to Camp Alexander Inc., Box 1022, Emporia, Kan. 66801.

The camp, which used to be considered way out in the country, is now flanked by a subdivision. Down the ridge, however, one can still see the patches of land where Jones' vegetables and fruits grew fat and shiny.

And atop the ridge is the old man's grave and marker.

Immortality? Perhaps Jones knew all along what it takes to attain that state. The words on his stone say simply:

Edward J. Alexander
The Children's Friend

Boston Corbett: A Nut Maligned

TOPEKA--It's too bad the Kansas legislature adjourned.

Otherwise we could expect some bombastic oratory and a tartly worded resolution condemning the defamation in Iowa of a former third assistant doorkeeper of the Kansas House of Representatives.

That doorkeeper was Boston Corbett, who could be seen standing around the legislative corridors in Topeka in the early months of 1877, his trusty .38-caliber pistol in his belt, the same weapon with which he had dispatched John Wilkes Booth 12 days after the assassination of President Abraham Lincoln.

The defamation of Corbett occurred last weekend in the *Des Moines Sunday Register*.

In a front page article, Josef Mossman noted the inadvertent placement of a photo of John Wilkes Booth in the place reserved for a photo of Donald Kaul, a *Register* columnist. Mossman interpreted the mix-up as triumphant vindication of the Finis Bates-Otto Eisenschiml theories -- theories that Booth escaped and Corbett killed someone else in the burning warehouse 113 years ago.

Further, Mossman suggests that it was Kaul who was killed and it is John Wilkes Booth who writes the column for the *Register*.

Eisenschiml, writing in 1937, never came close to naming whom Corbett killed, although he raised a lot of minute questions in his book "Why Was Lincoln Murdered?"

Bates, who in 1907 published a volume entitled "The Escape and Suicide of John Wilkes Booth," had answers -- mainly that Booth escaped from federal troops and headed west where he became a drunken and morphine-addicted housepainter named David E. George.

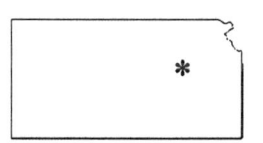

Bates said George frequently took to his deathbed and confessed he was John Wilkes Booth. After committing suicide in 1903 in Enid, Okla., George was promptly mummified, and for the next 40 years exhibited throughout the country.

Mossman paid a quarter in 1940 to see George's body, which he says looked like a petrified tree trunk. Mossman says the mummy resembled

Donald Kaul, the present-day columnist, as much as George or Booth or anyone else.

Once Booth-Kaul-Bates-Eisenschiml are dismissed, Mossman gets down to the real business at hand--Boston Corbett.

"Sgt. Corbett merits mention because he was one of the more nauseating characters in all history," Mossman wrote. "He claimed he fired the fatal shot, and took to the lecture platform to give his version of the shooting. When paying audiences failed to show up, he took to lecturing and preaching on street corners.

"He turned religious nut, castrated himself, and continued to make a nuisance of himself in various ways. In early 1876 he turned up in Mobile, Ala., where Edwin Booth (John's brother), was appearing during a tour of the southern states.

"Corbett's gall was disgusting beyond belief. He wrote to Edwin Booth asking for free tickets to the theater, saying he thought the actor surely wouldn't refuse him 'when I tell you that I'm the United States soldier that shot and killed your brother'."

That's pretty rough stuff. A check of newspaper files and some telephone calls indicated that Corbett, although he had problems, wasn't all that bad--odd, perhaps.

Albert T. Reid, the illustrator and cartoonist, writing in the July 1929 *Scribner's* magazine, termed Corbett "erratic." Reid knew Corbett when he was a youngster in Cloud County, Kan., where he said Corbett had taken up an 80-acre claim to get away from all the publicity surrounding the killing. Corbett, a hatter by trade, was not suited to farming, Reid said, because he brought a large number of sheep, most of which died and the rest of which moved into Corbett's cabin.

Reid said he knew of only one instance in which Corbett talked of the John Wilkes Booth killing--it was in front of a group of church ladies, and he stammered and barely got the story out.

So much for Corbett, the frustrated lecturer.

As for the self-inflicted mutilation, John Redjinski, curator of the Menninger Foundation Museum in Topeka, and a Corbett student, said it happened in 1856, before the Civil War, and apparently was prompted by Corbett's reading of the 18th and 19th chapters of the book of Matthew.

Reid described Corbett as a small, insignificant man with a scraggly beard, who always wore an old army cap. His hair was below his shoulders.

Reid claimed that Corbett once was hauled into court for breaking up a baseball game on Sunday. The game was not yet the national pastime. Tiring of the proceedings, Corbett produced his pistol and said:

"I've had enough of this. Court's adjourned."

And indeed it was, with the judge leading the flight for the exits.

Other history buffs pointed out some Kansans believed Corbett had been abused by the government and, as an apparent reward, they got him a job as third assistant doorkeeper at the House of Representatives in Topeka. Corbett immediately abandoned his claim and headed for the capital with the trusty .38 on his hip.

Unfortunately, he was the butt of jokes by his fellow employees. In mid-February 1877, when Corbett saw some of them holding a mock session in the chambers and, worst of all, invoking the Lord's name over it, he exploded. He pulled his gun, thereby adjourning the proceedings.

He was seized by police, tried for insanity the next day (the prosecutor was Charles Curtis, future vice-president of the United States), found guilty and sent to the asylum.

But Corbett apparently tired of confinement. In 1888 he stole a horse and escaped to Neodesha, Kan., where he told a friend he might go to Mexico.

"And after that he disappeared," said Redjinski. "Some say he went to Mexico; some say he drowned in the Kansas river. And there were reports that he became a patent medicine salesman."

It all just goes to show--defame a Kansan and you're likely to find an interesting character. Maybe a bit odd, but never, to use a synonym some Kansans use for Iowa, dull.

August 15, 1981

Novelist Lives Well with Rules

For a long heartbeat they stood thus, looking into each other's eyes. Then, as if by common consent, she was in his arms....Her head swam and her entire body tingled at the sensation of their meeting. There was no conscious thought in her except love for the man that held her.

Love's Captive by Samantha Lester

GIRARD, Kan. -- "I get so tired of virgins," Samantha Lester was saying. "You start 'em out as virgins, they gotta stay virgins."

Samantha Lester has a beard. Samantha also has hairy legs and drinks beer. Samantha was named after a wrestler.

But Samantha -- who actually is Lester V. "Sam" Roper, a Girard novelist -- plays by the rules as a writer of romance novels, and any paperback book buyer can see they have flooded the racks in recent years.

Absolute virginity to the final period on the final page is one of the rules.

There are others: the beautiful heroine must tremble against the threat of a fate worse than death, such as marrying a rich old man who is fat and mean; the time must be the early 1800s; a handsome stranger must appear as the love interest; the heroine's blouse can slip only to a point just below her shoulders; and, of course, good must triumph over evil and the heroine must be saved.

There are some exceptions, Roper says. If the novel has a contemporary setting, the heroine can be intimate with a man but must marry him.

Authors of such novels, he adds, must have English-sounding female names like Ann Dabney or Lucy Phillips Steward. Few, if any, romance novels are being penned by authors with names like Sadie Abramowicz.

Samantha Lester, of course, is perfect, says Roper, a former sailor, welder, barber, clerk-typist, munitions plant worker, college student at age 35 and now, at 50, the author of 20 novels. Four novels are romances written under Samantha's name.

Roper thinks Samantha Lester has a nice ring to it. Samantha, not Roper, was mobbed by reporters and magazine writers last month in Houston when he attended the annual meeting of the Romance Writers of America. "There were 400 women authors at the meeting," Roper says, "and me and a couple of other guys. I guess we sort of stuck out."

NBC News saw Roper and a film crew followed him back to Girard. He will be featured on a David Brinkley NBC News Magazine segment in September. He also will be in Fairway one day that month to autograph books at Rainy Day Books.

"I'm finally discovered after 15 years of writing," Roper says, and laughs.

He recalls that for almost half of those years, he didn't sell a thing and "could've papered a wall with rejection slips." But he never got discouraged. His wife, Kathleen, taught school; Roper became a self-described house husband, a rarity in a town like Girard, and kept writing, mostly thrillers and epics.

He says Kathleen and their two children, Sammy and Mary, would "buck me up if I got discouraged. They wanted me to write. And it was tough on the kids with people asking if their father was ever going to get a job."

"Then I got an agent, and in 32 days he sold most everything I'd written," Roper says. "I knew I'd sell. I knew I'd make it if I stuck with it."

About four years ago, Roper started writing romances set in England's Regency period. The reason? Money. Romances now account for two out of every five paperback books that are sold.

Roper says he hopes to write about one romance a month, interspersed with a thriller or two each year for Dell Books, his publisher. A new thriller, "The Reunion," will be out this fall, he says, and several movie studios already are looking at it. Several of his romances will be published in the next few months.

Roper can look at the covers of his books on the wall above the living room doorway and be frank enough to admit he'd been a lousy English student in high school.

"A few years ago, I saw Miss (Mildred) Heller, my old English teacher," he says, "and I asked her if she would have ever dreamed I'd be a novelist someday.

"She looked at me a minute, then looked out the window and started talking about the weather."

December 25, 1982

Age Casts New Light on Holiday

LEBANON, Mo. -- It's almost 400 miles from here to Ellsworth, Kan. It could be a million, judging from brief paragraphs appearing about Christmas in the newspapers of the two towns.

Earlier this month the *Lebanon Daily Record* ran a series of profiles of the needy in Laclede County. The profiles were numbered to give anonymity to those who had talked to Missouri Division of Aging caseworkers.

Two weeks later, the *Ellsworth Reporter* ran the traditional "Letters to Santa" from the children in the Geneseo, Kan., grade school. A lot of newspapers in Kansas and Missouri run similar letters.

Side by side, the content of those pages leaps out at the reader. It's not that there are no poor people in Ellsworth County nor any smiling children waiting expectantly for Santa Claus in Lebanon.

The key is age--the wonder of Christmas, evident in the children's letters. The profiles paint a bleaker picture. When you get older, practicality takes precedence, often to the point of laughter. Except when you think about it.

Take Lebanon's profile No. A16:

"A 73-year old lady and her 17-year old grandson live in the Falcon area. She requests light bulbs, washing powder, Sani-flush and Drano. All food items are requested as well as clothing for both. She could also use a raised toilet seat."

Or A17: "The elderly single woman in the Conway area could use any gift of long-sleeved clothing, size 16-18. She refuses to receive food stamps even though she would be eligible. Food needs are great for her. She could use firewood and a long-tailed coat. She has no family in this state and will have no one to share the holidays with."

Children think of other things. Christmas isn't keeping warm or cleaning the toilet bowl. That comes with age. Some letters published in the *Reporter*:

"Dear Santa,
I would like a Nerf football for

Christmas. I also want some hiking boots. I would really like to get a big backhoe to dig in the dirt with. I already have a dump truck. I would like some airplanes also. I would like some toy cars, a walkie-talkie, a shirt with E.T. on it, a semi, a race track, and a squirt gun.
   Love,
   Jawn Marsh.''

"Dear Santa,

How are your reindeers? I want a doll (a big one), an owl calculator, a new soccer ball, a coat, some skates and a play candle for my bedroom.
   Love,
   Bobbie Jo Long.''

"Dear Santa,

I have been a good boy this year. I would like a talking E.T., a Scooby-Doo and an Adventure game, a Tan-Tan, and R2D2, a C3PO and an E.T. bedroom set. My Mommy wants a mink coat. My Dad wants some more Alligator sweaters. My brother wants a Smurf rubber ball and my sister wants a doll--a ballerina. How's Rudolph?
   Love,
   Aaron Holm.''

In Lebanon, Division of Aging workers found a common theme in the requests from the needy. No Smurf balls, nothing with E.T. on it, nor any games. People asked for light bulbs, food, cleaning supplies and, in 11 of the 19 profiles, postage stamps. They still want to communicate, no matter what their circumstances.

Take A7: "This gentleman, age 81, lives alone. He would like some shoes, size EE; shirts, size 16; and food items such as meat, canned goods, fresh fruits and Christmas goodies. He also need Rolaids due to a health problem.''

Or A4: "This 64-year-old man lives in an old house with no running water. He would like help with repairs for his back porch.''

That's a simple Christmas wish. A repaired back porch.

A12, a 79-year-old man, asked for food and washing supplies. A1, a 79-year-old woman, wanted some throw rugs. A8, a widow, asked for some magazines and cookies.

Simple things. The kids in the Geneseo school asked for simple things, too--some bedroom slippers, a lampshade, two white rabbits, a new coat, and even earmuffs. Several inquired about Santa's health. And four promised to leave cookies and milk for Santa and Christmas Eve.

In Lebanon, A6 asked for some size 6 shoes. A2 told the caseworkers any Christmas gift could make her happy. And A15, an 80-year-old woman, broke down and asked for a little perfume. But first she asked for some Comet, Mr. Clean, Windex, and floor wax.

First things first. Especially on Christmas Day.

September 20, 1989

No Body Was Any the Wiser

FORT LEAVENWORTH-- This is the story of Abraham Johnston, who rode out of here in June 1846 as a captain of mounted dragoons, saw the as yet untrammeled West, then came home almost six years later disguised as a cookstove.

All in all, Capt. Johnston--a big, affable officer who was educated at West Point--is no more than a footnote in history. Yet in a larger sense, his story, like others before it and doubtless others hence, proves what most everybody knows about the government: what could go wrong usually does.

Capt. Johnston was born in Upper Piqua, Ohio, in 1815, one of 15 children. Families back then were somewhat larger.

Piqua, by the way, would have its name appropriated years later by some Kansas settlers from a Woodson County town. And years after that Piqua, Kan., would gather its own measure of immortality as the birthplace of Buster Keaton.

Anyway, when the Mexican War broke out, the captain and the Fort Leavenworth dragoons headed west, helped occupy Santa Fe, N.M. without a fight, then marched on to California to bring the blessings of the American government to that region.

A problem arose. Some Californians found the American annexation, well, rude. Thus when the Americans approached San Diego on Dec. 6, 1846, a paramilitary bunch called, naturally, the "Californios" resisted at a suburb called San Pascual.

There they fatally shot Capt. Johnston in the head, mortally stabbed troopers with the lances they favored and generally gave the invaders a very bloody nose.

No matter. California was conquered, and the dead were buried. And that seemed to be that.

Except....

Three years later Johnston's father decided his son should be buried in Upper Piqua. Arrangements were made over the next two years by slow mail--about the same as today, or so it seems--and eventually what was left of Capt. Johnston was dug up, placed in a small container, and transported north to San Francisco to await the next ship headed around Cape Horn.

In April 1852, Capt. Johnston was reburied in Ohio. A big marker was erected. The only disquieting memory of the affair was how heavy the coffin was.

But then there seemed to be an explanation--lead-lined caskets were common then. Or lime was packed in the casket to keep the odor down during shipping. Still, some said, there hadn't been all that much left of Capt. Johnston, had there?

Six months later and 2,300 miles to the west, the San Francisco papers were screaming about the horrendous murder that had been discovered near the docks.

A fire had occurred in a stove factory warehouse. Boxes were removed to save them. Once the fire was out, some idler opened the boxes. In two he found stoves, in the third was a badly decomposed body.

The next day, the papers were less excited. The body, they said, was of a U.S. Army officer who had fallen at San Pascual six years earlier. Through some shipping mix-up, the box had been consigned to the bowels of a warehouse amid the stoves. Although the San Francisco paper never mentioned the officer's name, it had to be Capt. Johnston. He was the only officer disinterred for shipment home.

And after that, silence--both in the press and in Army records. In a 1948 book called *Lances at San Pascual*, author Arthur Woodward theorized that the government--to spare the Johnston family more pain--quietly reburied the bones somewhere in the San Francisco area. Out of sight, out of mind.

And underneath the fine marble monument in Upper Piqua?

"What else," said Woodward. "A rusting stove."

July 5, 1985

Village Returning to Normal

RICHMOND, Mo. -- This Ray County town of 6,000 people stopped being on the forefront of what the electronic media call "the global village" Thursday.

John L. Testrake, the pilot of Trans World Airlines Flight 847, was home. With his arrival over, two big satellite transmitting dishes were leaving.

For the immediate future Richmond will be a receiver of news, not an origination point. You talk to people here on the square and they say that's fine. Richmond's had enough of that, what with television reporters camped out on the courthouse lawn, telephone calls from all over the world coming in bunches to Howard Hill, editor at the *Richmond Daily News*, and reporters asking, time and again, whether a resident personally knew Mr. Testrake.

Still, there are a bunch of little facts about Richmond, things that never made the papers back east or the television shows.

Some of the facts, but not all, show a certain dichotomy about Richmond, especially when the news paints it as a "typical" Midwestern town. The horror and fanaticism of the Middle East, while seemingly news, aren't strangers to Richmond.

For instance, Bob Ford is buried here. Mr. Ford was "the dirty little coward who shot Mr. Howard," the latter being Jesse Woodson James. In the eyes of the state of Missouri in 1882, Mr. James was a terrorist, except such people were called "outlaws" then. Mr. Ford had a contract on Jesse, much like contracts people are talking about now to bring 847's hijackers to justice.

And William Anderson, also known as "Bloody Bill," is in a grave here. He was a terrorist pure and simple, taking soldiers off a train in Centralia, Mo., lining them up and shooting them dead. Mr. Anderson also encouraged his men to cut the ears off Union soldiers and string them on their bridles. Or tie prisoners to trees near hog lots. That was a slow way to die.

Naturally the local newspaper, then edited by Col. John Edwards, thought the excesses of Bill and Jesse were overblown; they were just poor, misunderstood boys, hounded by an oppressive government for the sacred "Lost Cause" of the Confederacy.

A whole bunch of Mormons are also buried here, including two men who witnessed the transcribing of the Book of Mormon from the plates Joseph Smith received. The Mormons' religious zeal--proselytizing among the Indians, for instance--angered certain Jackson Countians enough that they murdered them.

So there're those things. And here the other night, waiting for the Testrake motorcade to pass, was Everett Lauck, Ray County circuit clerk. Mr. Lauck, an open-faced man, allowed he had been watching a lot of television news lately, especially one of the Kansas City news anchors who reminds him of a young gunner in his tank back when he was with the 5th Armored Division in France and Germany in World War II.

"That anchor looks just like that gunner," Mr. Lauck was saying.

The gunner and two other crewmen were killed when then Sgt. Lauck's Sherman took a direct hit on the turret from a German 88-millimeter gun. Mr. Lauck wasn't scratched.

"Well," said Mr. Lauck, the words coming in bits and pieces, almost forced, "ordnance welded up the hole. . . . For weeks we scrubbed and cleaned, getting teeth and gums and hair out of the inside. It smelled so bad. Finally they gave us a whole new turret."

Eventually Mr. Lauck came home, stepping off the train a few miles from Richmond in Henrietta, at midnight, Oct. 15, 1945. He remembers his discharge was signed by a woman named Mary A. Pickett, a clerk at Jefferson Barracks over in St. Louis.

And was there anybody to meet him, to welcome him home?

Mr. Lauck, looking at the activities in the square as people waited for the motorcade, looked surprised at the question.

"Oh, no," he said. "Just my folks."

March 17, 1984

Klan Rode Roughshod in Kansas

TOPEKA -- Name the state in which the following happened:

Bands of men invaded Protestant churches in the midst of services and demanded money--what they called "donations."

A mayor was beaten severely for refusing to rent a building to the group.

The state's largest newspaper refused advertisements denouncing the criminal acts of the organization.

The lame-duck governor refused to speak out against the group, his lieutenant governor actively sought the band's endorsement in the primary election, and the other party's candidate kept his mouth shut about the whole thing.

Twelve hundred members of the group marched in the state capital. Other members won local elections and wrote letters threatening whippings to "less desirable elements" of various communities.

Well, obviously, such things just had to happen in one of the Southern states.

Not quite. All the above happened 60 years ago in Kansas. And the group was the Ku Klux Klan, 100,000 strong in the Sunflower State between 1922 and 1924 by most estimates.

The Klan has crept back into the news lately. There were allusions to the Klan being active in an area in southwest Missouri where the Mayor of Weaubleau was shot to death. No link to the Klan, however, was made. And this week there were reports of a "mock" Klan rally among some soldiers at Fort Riley, Kan., although that apparently was a prank.

The Klan has largely faded from Kansas. But 60 years ago the Klan was a force, burning crosses almost nightly in Wichita, Cottonwood Falls and other localities.

And there was nothing subtle about the Klan when it wrote to C.E. St. John, superintendent of schools in Arkansas City, suggesting that though it probably was too late in the current year to make major changes, he should seriously consider hiring "100 percent Protestant teachers for the next school year."

Klan No. 8 of Caney wrote on its letterhead to roller rink and dance hall owner William Liberman that "400 of the best element in this vicinity are against you and can you afford to take the chance? We warn but once."

Looking at the voluminous files, legal papers, correspondence and Klan paraphernalia held by the Kansas State Historical Society, the message the Klan sent wasn't the virulent anti-black message it has been associated with in recent years.

In Kansas, at least, the Klan's real dislikes seemed to have been Jews and Catholics. Of the two, the majority of the propaganda seemed aimed at the "Romish." Catholics, the Klan was always saying, thought that Protestant women were "loose," and that anybody who didn't swear fealty to Rome "should be drawn and quartered...impaled and hung up for the crows to eat."

The Klan, which used a lot of reverse psychology, was not in the least ecumenical.

It was not a proud period for a state settled 70 years earlier to blunt slavery or the one that sent the highest proportion of any state into Union ranks in the fight to make men free.

Something in a lot of Kansans' psyche seemed to respond to the Klan. It may have been nativism, the economic depression already on the prairie, a distrust of foreigners (thus Catholics) and, maybe more importantly, a desire to reassert control over their lives. Five years earlier they had been hauled, unwillingly, into a European war, and really nothing seemed to have changed over there for all their sacrifices.

One man, however, did much to drive the Klan from Kansas. William Allen White, the Emporia newspaperman, threw his hat in the ring for governor, campaigned for six weeks, gave 106 speeches and spent $474.60, a pittance by today's standards. He got 103,000 votes and ran third.

But just by running, Mr. White did enough, mainly through derision. In his speeches he exposed the Klansmen for the frauds they were, describing them as "gargoyles in nighties and flour sacks."

Not many Kansas Klansmen wanted to be described as wearing "nighties." After 1924, for a variety of reasons, not the least of which was Mr. White, the Klan went quickly from the Kansas scene, its detritus largely contained in the faded papers kept at the Historical Society in Topeka.

August 23, 1985

Mailboxes Now Going Hog Wild

SEDALIA, Mo. -- You wonder sometimes about the government? Think it's intrusive? Meddlesome? Sticking its nose where it doesn't belong?

Listen to Ron Frazier, who along with his stepdad, Bill Coon, make up most of what's called Coon Manufacturing and Distributing Co. in Spickard, Mo., up north of Trenton.

Spickard, by the way, was originally Spickardsville until the first train came through and somebody had to climb up and saw off the "sville" part of the sign at the railroad station because it blocked the departing train. Progress, back then, had its price.

"We wanted to put the door of our mailboxes in the front," Mr. Frazier says. "The postal people made us put it in the ah, what's it called? Oh, yeah, posterior."

Mr. Frazier, 21, chose that last word carefully. In Spickard, at least in mixed company, words like posterior are rarely used, folks eschewing words with fancy Latin roots for more earthy, Anglo-Saxon ones, which seem more direct and express the speaker's ideas more succinctly. One syllable words.

Mr. Frazier and Mr. Coon, being progressive businessmen, are at the Missouri State Fair this week selling hog feeders, hog pans, farrowing crate dividers and pig brooders, all made of what Mr. Frazier calls "space-age plastic."

Ditto for the material they're using in their mailboxes -- hard, tough plastic made at the plant in Spickard.

The mailboxes, which have been around about a year and are selling well, are different. They don't look like the aluminum-colored breadboxes you usually see in the country. First off, they're plastic. But the real difference is their shape.

One model is a John Deer tractor. The other two are a rooting pig and a solid looking steer -- really maybe a bull -- in sort of a show-pose.

Mailboxes.

"Add a charming, rural touch to the yard or roadside with a new mailbox," is how the promotional literature Mr. Frazier has been handing out describes the mailboxes. The price is $45 at the fair this week, a special from the regular $59.95. For an extra 10 bucks, Mr. Frazier or Mr. Coon will custom paint your pig or steer to resemble your particular breed -- a Duroc or a Hereford, a Chester White or an Angus.

The tractor mailbox comes in just one style, though, John Deere green.

"Naturally," Mr. Frazier says, "the door on the tractor has to be at the back because that's where tractors are biggest. That just makes sense."

As for the pig and steer, Mr. Frazier admits the rear ends of such animals are bigger but really not by all that much. The original idea was to have the door sort of hinge at the lower part of the animal's chest. The head would drop down and the mail would be put in. Then the mailman would close it and a Hampshire pig or a Hereford steer would be looking at him.

Straight in the eye.

But no, says Mr. Frazier, the postal people figured with the head down, the mail carrier would have to reach in too far, maybe three or four more inches.

"They told us we had to put the door in, ah, the back part of the pig or steer, you know, because it was bigger back there and it wouldn't be as far to reach.

"So we did it. Who are we to fight the government?"

And that's the way the mailboxes are. The hinge is on top of the hip of the pig and steer. The red flag is on the right side. The pig and steer, obviously, face away from the roadside.

And the mail carrier, obviously, after he delivers the mail, gets a long hard look at the part of the pig or steer which, if you think about it, sort of sums up what kind of mentality you have to have to write such postal regulations.

"Pretty soon we'll have a new model that opens the same way," Mr. Frazier says.

What'll it be?

"Why a horse," Mr. Frazier says, smiling.

December 23, 1990

Father & Daughter Extol the Tourist Virtues of Kansas

INMAN, Kan.-- Mil Penner tells this story:

"Friends of mine moved to Wichita. Naturally, the Welcome Wagon came. And then a notice of a meeting to acquaint new arrivals with what Wichita and the rest of the state had to offer.

"My friends went. The meeting was pretty short. Somebody got up and told them about a couple of things they could do in Wichita. Plays. Music. And then they got this. Right between the eyes.

" 'If you want anything more in the way of culture or things to do,' my friends heard, 'you'll probably have to go to Denver or Kansas City.' "

Mil still gets an edge to his voice when he tells the story. For him, it's kind of a summation of what's wrong with Kansans' ideas about Kansas. My Lord, he says, haven't they ever looked around their state?

For instance:

Theater-- the Kechi playhouse; the Ric Averill Players near Valley Falls; theater in Pavilion Park in Manhattan; Flint Hills Opry in Burlington; and Brown Grand Theater in Concordia. And that's just for starters.

Festivals-- Bluegrass, Czech, Kickapoo, Maple Leaf, Messiah, Threshing, Millfest and Tulip are eight of 17 Mil can tick off.

Art-- There's Pete Felten, a Hays sculptor who has a gallery there. Or there's Stan Herd murals, one right here in Inman, another in Dodge City. Herd's the fellow who creates art out of farm fields. Or there's Ern and Lucille Hett, who weld copper into art south of Marion.

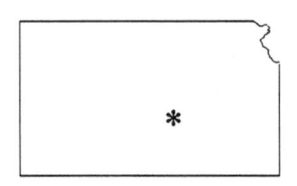

Mil and his daughter, Marci Penner, are sort of missionaries to the uninformed of Kansas. What they do is reveal parts of the state that some know about and ignore, and others have never heard of but find absolutely fascinating.

What Mil and Marci have done is put together a book called *Kansas Weekend Guide* (available in bookstores or from Route 1, Inman, Kan. 67546) that lists hundreds and hundreds of things--from American Indian monuments to the Wizard of Oz, old-fashioned hardware stores to still-working soda fountains, museums to art galleries.

"We've only scratched the surface," says Marci. "There's just so much."

So far, father and daughter have sold 10,000 of the books.

And how has it been received? Listen to Mil:

"In early November we had a party out here on the farm," he says. "We invited people who are in the book--museum curators, cafe owners, craftsmen, bed-and-breakfast operators, and the best kind of all, people you can just call up or visit with and have them tell you about their part of Kansas.

"Well, it was a rainy, miserable day. But you know how many showed up? A thousand. Maybe more."

Mil is almost evangelistic about Kansas. Along with Carol Schmidt, he's published two stunning picture books, one about Kansas, the other about the prairie from Minnesota to Texas, Missouri to the Rockies. Kansas, naturally, got its share in that book.

For *Weekend*, he and Marci hit the road, seeking out everything imaginable--from the 55-year-old amateur performance contest staged on summer Saturday nights in Thayer to the underground city beneath Ellinwood.

Oddly, Mil's professions, up until now, have been somewhat removed from publishing. Try earthmoving, farming and selling irrigation equipment.

Marci majored in radio and television at the University of Kansas and returned not long ago from Pennsylvania, where she was a school counselor.

No matter. They both love Kansas.

"I think our next book will deal more with events than just places," says Mil.

"And we've got some dandies already," says Marci. "There's a town out west that come Christmas gets all the farm machinery and cement trucks and stock trailers and combines, decks them with lights, and has a parade."

Now that, says Marci, is an event. Not exactly big city. But maybe something even better. Maybe Kansas.

July 31, 1987

The Day Gangsters Visited

ORONOGO, Mo. -- A hot summer afternoon. Center Creek, south of town, was full of kids beating the 97-degree heat.

Uptown -- or what's left of it -- about a half dozen persons were gathered at Jim's Gas and Grocery. It, a tavern down the street, and the post office are about all that's left of Oronogo, once a town of 2,000 people with a wide main street full of Saturday night crowds that made walking on the sidewalks difficult. There were even trolleys to Alba and Joplin, Webb City and Purcell, Neck City and Carl Junction.

Originally the town was named Minersville. But another town had that moniker, so somebody, legend has it, figured there was either ore here or not. So let's see.

"Oronogo."

And there was ore here--zinc and lead in unbelievable quantities. The ore was mined for years until government price supports went off and the shafts, one by one, were closed. The miners went away. Oronogo dwindled to about 500 people, most of them commuters to Joplin now.

Up at Jim's this day the talk, at least briefly, was of a new catalpa fish bait made out of the worms that crawl on catalpa trees.

Naturally, the stuff's called "Catalpa Worm Bait." It looks like a brick of oozing black tar. The store owner, Jim Hargis, gets the stuff out of Crestline, Kan., and said it's terrific -- catches catfish like crazy.

"I've only had one complaint," he said. "And that guy complains about everything."

It was one of those country store conversations, about what's going on, the good fishing in Center Creek when it's cooler, and ain't that bait ugly stuff.

"If you want to know about Oronogo, go see Don Board," somebody said. "He'll tell you about Bonnie and Clyde."

Board was over at the Masonic hall puttering around. Sure, he had time to talk--in fact, sit down here on the stoop, out of the sun, and we'll visit.

Board's lived here all his life. He and his parents moved into the house up by the water tower when he was 6 months old. That was 75 and a half years ago.

"I know where everything is in that house," Board said. "You can believe that."

Bonnie and Clyde? Well, sure. Board recalled all that happened in the early 1930s when two men walked into the bank here, a bank now long gone. Doc Norton -- no, he wasn't a real doctor, just had that nickname -- looked up.

One man, thought to be Clyde Barrow, demanded money. Right off Norton, who ran the bank, set off the alarm, which rang in the garage directly opposite the bank. In the garage were a whole bunch of rifles and shotguns.

Board saw it all. He was right across the street sitting in the barber's chair getting his hair cut. He saw the men go in, one converse with Doc, then Doc duck behind the counter, and that's when the shooting started. Miraculously, no one was hurt.

"I don't know if they got any money or not," Board said. "They came out of the bank and the guys in the garage came out with guns, and bullets were flying all over the place. The barber and I got on the floor."

The robbers escaped, abandoning their bullet-riddled car west of town. People always said it was Bonnie Parker and Clyde Barrow because someone saw a homely woman who looked like Bonnie waiting in another car west of town about the time the bank was robbed.

And the identifications were reinforced about a week later when the famous Bonnie and Clyde shoot-out occurred in Joplin.

"I do remember that after we got off the floor the barber was shaking so much that he could hardly hold the scissors," Board said.

Then Board talked of other things -- the saloons and churches that existed almost side by side, the Oronogo town baseball team that used to whup up on nines all over the area, and how on Saturday he, little Don Board, would get a penny from his father to spend on as much candy as 1 cent would buy.

And how the town just sort of faded away before his eyes. Nothing dramatic, mind you, but one day there just wasn't much left. Being a mailman, Board saw it all.

And it's funny, Board added, how you remember the little, seemingly insignificant things. Like the incline the trolley had to go up on its way to Alba and Purcell.

"As kids, we'd get some axle grease, coat the rails, and that trolley would just sit on that hill and go nowhere," said Board, laughing at the memory.

"Now why would I remember something like that after all these years?"

'Bleeding, Purging, Puking'

HUTCHINSON, Kan. -- Think traveling these days is a hassle? Angered about airline delays, lost bags, overbooked flights?

And the other things? The white-knuckles takeoffs and landings, reports of near collisions, and tales about burnt- out air traffic controllers?

Terrible, you say.

You want terrible?

Listen to Dr. Peter Olch, a medical historian from Bethesda, Md. If you think traveling is rough now, go back to the good old Santa Fe Trail days between the 1820s and the 1880s.

Saturday morning Olch, a tall, balding fellow, stood in front of 300 people who'd just eaten breakfast and launched into his topic, "Bleeding, Purging and Puking in the Southwestern Fur Trade and Along the Santa Fe Trail." At the end of an hour Olch had elicited several gasps and more than a few groans from those attending a symposium on the trail at Hutchinson Community College.

Olch's thesis was that folks heading west a century and a half ago weren't just taking a two-hour trip in the friendly skies. Their trip would take months. On that trip there was a good chance they'd get hurt or sick. And once that happened, Katy bar the door.

It was so bad, Olch said, that Brigham Young warned Mormons, "If you are sick, leave the surgeons alone if you want to live."

Olch said those were the days of "heroic medicine," the physicians' term then for "vigorous and violent therapy." That include purgatives, bleedings, and blistering. It meant igniting gunpowder on top of a snake bite and performing amputations with a key-hole saw and practicing surgery with a Green River knife--an instrument considerably larger than a scalpel.

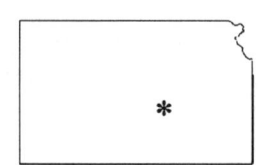

There was cholera and malaria, dysentery and typhoid, smallpox and diphtheria. A common treatment for the latter was to coat sandburs with tallow, tie a string to them and then force them down the patient's throat. Once the tallow dissolved, the sandburs were jerked out, bringing up the diphtheritic membrane that had blocked the throat. William Bent, trader and occasional resident of Westport, underwent that treatment and somehow survived.

Gastro-intestinal maladies were common on the trail, many caused by what's thought now to have been poor camp sanitation. The great mystery for a medical historian about the westward migration, Olch said, is how the immigrants tended to their basic functions. That aspect was never mentioned in all the diaries or journals that the travelers left behind.

The catchall cure was calomel, or mercurous chloride, and it was used copiously for everything from intermittent fever (malaria) to diarrhea. A common side effect of calomel was gangrene of the jaw, not a pleasant affliction anywhere, let alone somewhere south of Lakin, Kan., heading for the Cimarron cutoff.

And oddly, Olch said, the leading cause of death on the Santa Fe wasn't Indian raids. No, most people died falling off moving wagons. Next came accidental gunshot wounds, stampeding livestock, immigrants attacking each other, lightning, drowning, and suicide.

Then, and only then, did the Indians come riding over the hills yelling for scalps.

It wasn't easy then. It wasn't 1987.

So next time a flight is delayed or luggage is misdirected, relax. Think, but only briefly, please, about the sandbur cure for diphtheria.

July 25, 1990

Eads 'Boys' Have What It Takes to Fix Anything

HOPE, Mo. -- This sound familiar?

Something breaks and you take it in to be fixed. First you have to get a number and then stand in line before dealing with a bored, gum-chewing clerk. He or she says they'll call you. When? In a few weeks. Maybe they can fix it, maybe not. Still, no matter what, there'll be a hefty charge just to look at what's broken.

Down here in rural Osage County, for as long as anyone can remember, things have been different. If something's busted you take it to the Eads boys who live north of here. No numbers. Twinkling eyes instead of exasperated looks. And what if they can't get a part?

"Well, I reckon we can just make that part," was what one of the Eads boys would say. And before long what was busted was good as new. Probably better.

The Eads aren't exactly "boys" anymore. Fred is 82. Philomenea, 77, his wife of 60-plus years, told a visitor Saturday that he was out back. And Fred's brother, Oliver, 92, who lives with them? "Oh, he's resting," Philomenea said.

Indeed, Fred, was down behind the house, a screwdriver and file in one hand, a 12-gauge shotgun in the other.

"Looks pretty good, doesn't it?" said Fred, eyeing the weapon. "Actually this is parts of 12 shotguns I've had over the years. Got to thinking, why let all those old parts just lie around? So I fiddled some and came up with this. All it needs is just a little oil."

Fiddling. That's what the Eads boys have done all these years. Fiddling with stuff most people now would throw away. And farming, running cows on 500 acres on either side of Route J.

Not long ago they sold 300 of those acres, the part called the old home place. That part was bought all those years ago by their daddy, Nathan, who incidentally, fiddled with broken things, too. But they still have the acreage on the north side of the road, land they keep mowed with their old

Farmall tractors that have cranks, not batteries.

They get some Social Security. Plus rent from land used for haying. They don't need much. There's not a credit card among them. No telephone. The television set, Fred says, hasn't been on in weeks. "We got enough for beans," Fred said. "Beans do us fine."

And they get a little something from fixing things, mainly old guns and clocks now.

"Don't fix things like we used to," Fred said. "Getting too old. Used to fiddle with cars, but I get all stove up trying to crawl under them."

In fact, Oliver hardly does any fiddling now. His health is fairly good. But he is 92 year old. And almost stone deaf.

About then, Oliver came out of the bedroom, looking refreshed, and commenting on the weather. Darnedest year he's ever seen, he told a visitor. Floods one week, drought the next. Can you figure it?

No, said the visitor, looking at wonderful photograph on the wall, one taken of Oliver and Fred 20-odd years ago. Both are sitting on a stoop, each holding a muzzle-loading rifle. The picture looks like it could have been taken in 1850, not 1970.

"Muzzle-loading?" Fred said. "Now that's what we've both always loved. Bet I've shot a wagonful of black powder in my life. My brother the same."

Both men still belong to an informal muzzle-loading group that gets together on occasions and fills the hills and hollows along Highway 89 near here with noise and smoke.

Occasionally Fred will take the .36-caliber muzzle-loader he made in 1933 and fire it. It has a 4-foot barrel, one he drilled and rifled by hand. "Shoots good," Fred said, hefting what has become, in his lifetime, an antique.

But muzzle-loading and fixing things are only part of what people here talk about when they mention the Eads boys. What strikes people is that the brothers and Philomenea have held on and haven't, like most of us, sold out to all the modern way. And they mention one particular sight they see on hot summer evenings when they drive past the Eads boys' place.

There'll be Fred and his wife and Oliver all sitting out front, beneath their old cedar tree, two of them listening to the sound of the woods, Oliver maybe watching the stars make their transit across the sky, all waiting for the air to cool before going to bed. Three people in front of a small white house on a Missouri back road. Together. Just a little thing.

But who does that anymore?

September 15, 1989

Vanished Road with Vital Link

FULTON, Kan. -- Earlier this week Kansas officials made a big whoop-de-do over the slated reconstruction of U.S. 69 in Johnson County.

The cost for a few miles of resurfacing and bridge work? Millions.

That same afternoon, three miles east of here, a mud-splattered station wagon drove down a soupy trace hard by what used to be the village of Barnesville, Kan., a place that's dwindled to four corners, a few houses and a cemetery.

"We call this the magic mile," said Arnold Schofield, driver of the station wagon and historian at the Fort Scott (Kan.) National Historic Site. In the back, Ora Stuart, a retired math and science teacher and an old forward observer in the field artillery, nodded.

That mile, now an obscure Bourbon County road, is used mostly by farm trucks, combines and tractors. Its cost, originally? How about $287.50? For one whole mile.

That price says a couple of things about inflation and how old the road is.

"As far as we know, this is the only part of the Fort Leavenworth to Fort Scott military road that is overlaid with a 'modern road,' " Schofield said. "In fact, I'd bet it looks almost exactly how the old military road did -- narrow, muddy in wet weather, and following the high ground."

The military road construction started in 1838, as the federal government's answer to the Indians who had been removed to the Kansas and Oklahoma territories. It was what one writer has termed a physical symbol of "American apartheid." The Indians would be on reservations to the west, whites on the farms to the east. Voila, the "Indian problem" would be solved.

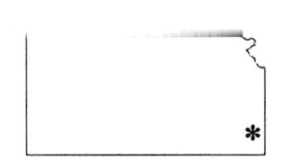

And the road was no small-scale solution. Patrolled by soldiers to keep the Indians in and the whites out, it would stretch from Fort Snelling in Minnesota to Fort Jesup northwest of New Orleans.

So the road was a big deal, large enough in people's minds to foster the myth that U.S. 69 -- from Minneapolis to Texas -- was built atop what once was a pathway through the wilderness.

Not so, Stuart said. His calculations, done with old maps, collated against modern topographic ones and using measurement increments of one-eighth mile, show that -- at least in this part of Kansas -- the military road was generally two to four miles east of the current highway.

Another unexpected discovery has been that tiny parts of the road went through Bates and Cass County, Mo.

All in all, what Stuart, using his old artillery plotting skills, and Schofield, a voracious reader of obscure 19th century diaries and footnotes, have discovered is remarkable.

Stuart always had hope. The mystery of the road's location had obsessed him for years. He knew what had happened. In the late 19th century, with the Indians gone, the coming of more settlers, the building of railroads and newer, more direct farm-to-market roads, the old military road just sort of disappeared. Oh, people remembered it. But as the years passed, nobody could say just exactly where it was.

The original surveyor's map was just one thin line, uncoordinated with landmarks. The mile markers set out in the fall of 1838 -- piles of rocks -- were long gone.

But in the archives of the Kansas State Historical Society in Topeka, Stuart and Schofield found an all-but-forgotten 1857 survey done in anticipation of Kansas becoming a state. The survey had the coordinates, the latitude and longitude markers, and all the rest. Plus the military road. Using U.S. Geological Survey maps, the maps were compared and the original route laid out.

And Stuart, 72, found more than lines on paper. He showed a visitor a cut near the Little Osage River bridge south of Barnesville.

"Now, there isn't enough drainage here to create that kind of slope to the river," he said. "It's man-made. There was a ford here. You can see it."

Schofield said the road is a little-known part of history and in its own way as dramatic as the Santa Fe or Oregon trails. Over the road traveled the wagons laden with Indian allotments, the soldiers headed for the Mexican War, the land-hungry settlers, the guerrillas who turned this part of Missouri and Kansas into a preview of Vietnam, Civil War prisoners of war, even the newly freed slaves. For 30 years it was a busy, congested interstate highway. Then it was gone.

"We have accounts of supply trains," Schofield said. "How long were they? Well, if you stood by this road it'd take a single train six hours to pass you by.

"That long."

August 31, 1982

The Gospel According to Mahan

BOONVILLE, Mo. -- DeWitt, Mo., is up-river from here, a quiet town that ought to put up a sign saying: "The Rev. W.D. Mahan was inspired here."

Well, not quite in DeWitt. Mr. Mahan was stranded on a steamboat out in the Missouri River, icebound from an early freeze in the fall of 1856. While waiting for the ice to thaw, the preacher struck up a conversation with a gentleman named H.D. Whydaman, who identified himself as a German scholar.

The conversation, naturally, turned to the Bible. Mr. Whydaman revealed to Mr. Mahan that certain rare manuscripts in the Vatican library pertaining to the life of Christ were just waiting to be discovered by a Cumberland Presbyterian such as Mr. Mahan.

Mr. Mahan pondered the ramifications of Mr. Whydaman's statement for a while, once he got back to his pulpit in Boonville. In fact, he pondered for 27 years. Later a less-than-charitable Missouri newspaper was to charge that Mr. Mahan learned the art of waiting during the years he spent in Eastern penitentiaries for various scams before coming to Missouri and passing himself off as a preacher.

Anyway, in 1883, Mr. Mahan took off for Rome and points east to unearth the writings of Caiaphas, Pontius Pilate, Herod and others -- primary source materials, as historians would say.

Mr. Mahan apparently was a terrific researcher. Once in Rome (critics later would say he got no further than Rome, Ga.), he managed to come up with everything he needed in just three days. Good stuff, too, including Pontius Pilate's original reports on the trial and execution of Christ, Herod's writings on the same matter, even related documents from the Roman Senate.

No copies either. Mr. Mahan got the real McCoy, all dated in the first century.

Mr. Mahan didn't dilly-dally at the Vatican. He immediately went to Constantinople and in a couple of days uncovered all sorts of Jewish records relating to Christ's life.

Both in Rome and Constantinople Mr. Mahan managed to get the discovered documents translated immediately so that he knew what he had. Apparently, it was all in knowing where to look. Somehow, as busy as he was -- researching, getting translations and then writing it all down -- he managed to jot a note to his wife saying he'd be home soon.

By the fall of 1883, Mr. Mahan was back in Boonville getting his book ready for the publisher. He titled it, *Archaeological Writings of the Sanhedrin and the Talmud of the Jews*, and then he added a subtitle, *The Most Interesting History Ever Read By Man*.

Mr. Mahan reported that he was publishing the book because Jewish scholars wanted to suppress the information he'd found. He was kinder to Catholic historians. They just hadn't gotten around to it, he said.

The contents of the book left many people aghast. Gamaliel, sent by the Sanhedrin to interview Joseph and Mary about their child, Jesus, reported that Joseph was "tall and ugly," with unkempt hair and "vicious eyes."

Gamaliel went on: "He (Joseph) is very disagreeable to his family....Upon the whole I should call them a third-rate family."

Then Mr. Mahan trotted out Caiaphas' report to Sanhedrin on the execution of Christ, saying that Jesus "had no education, comparatively speaking. He was full of nervous excitement, all of which went to inspire his hearers with enthusiasm. He took little care of his health or person; cared not for his own relatives.

"He traveled mostly on foot in the company of his disciples and some suspicious women and lived on the charity of his friends."

Mr. Mahan said his research had been relatively easy since most of the materials were as "plain as the advertisements of patent medicines on a plank fence," an odd way of describing biblical research.

The book hit the religious community like a bombshell. Eventually it was translated into 20 languages. But within a year a St. Louis newspaper called Mr. Mahan a literary pirate, accusing him of lifting whole sections of Lew Wallace's *Ben Hur* and claiming authorship. Mr. Mahan, not one to take criticism lightly, claimed that he was the real author of *Ben Hur* and that Mr. Wallace was merely his agent.

Archaeological Writings of the Sanhedrin and the Talmud of the Jews caused so much controversy, at least until the end of the century, that books were published giving reasons why Mr. Mahan's book shouldn't have been published. Finally in the 1930s, a university professor declared the book a hoax, something that the Boonville residents who knew the preacher could have told him all along.

September 17, 1986

Hang 'Em If You Got 'Em

WICHITA -- Back between 1883 and 1895 a division of the federal district court here in Wichita dealt with crimes committed in northern and western Oklahoma, known than as the Indian Territory.

A similar function for the no-man's land was performed by another federal court over in Fort Smith, Ark. It, however, had as judge a former Missouri congressman named Isaac Parker, who gained a measure of notoriety for himself and his court because of the frequency of men mounting the gallows there. The Fort Smith jurisdiction was mainly eastern Oklahoma.

The court here, like that of Judge Parker's, did not deal with high society. When miscreants were apprehended at places like Noble or Guthrie or Oklahoma City, they were packed off to Wichita. The records of that old court are now at the Kansas City branch of the National Archives.

Interestingly, the records have a correlation to 1986. In its years of existence, the Wichita court prosecuted one crime above all others -- drug dealing, i.e., the "Introduction of Liquor to Indians." Like it or not, some of our great-grandfathers were pushers.

And some of the crimes back then seem to jump out of today's headlines. Remember a week ago when Lester Hayes, the Los Angeles Raiders defensive back, was accused of trying to gouge out the eyes of Denver Broncos' Vance Johnson?

Mr. Johnson and Mr. Hayes had nothing on Anderson Bailey and Robert Dorsey, who were taking their ease at Guthrie's Woodbine bar March 8, 1890.

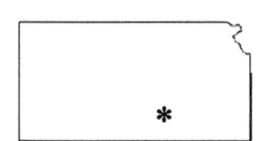

The drinks were to patch up some "difficulties." But apparently, in the midst of happy hour, Mr. Bailey took exception to something Mr. Dorsey said. As Mr. Dorsey later testified:

"He said, 'Have another drink,' and as I reached for it, he shouted and struck me. We rolled onto the floor, and I got on top of him.

"Then he yelled and spit my ear at me."

Mr. Dorsey said until that moment he had not missed his left ear, a fact that surprised him, as well as the patrons of the Woodbine. "When the fight was finished, Dorsey was minus an ear," marveled one G.H. Shirley.

For that breach of social etiquette, Mr. Bailey, who doubtless was of the stuff middle linebackers later would be made of, was charged with "mayhem."

In those days, the federal bench also probed into various private areas of citizens' lives.

A Mr. B. and a Mrs. U. of Oklahoma City were charged with breaking the federal law concerning adultery after being seen in a certain compromising position near a creek. Both were hauled off to Wichita, jailed briefly and then subjected to a public court hearing. Which, considering Victorian sensibilities, must have been worse than the chiggers.

Yet the words of the old records are what is most appealing. Take, for example, this indictment for murder:

"On the sixth of August, 1889, L.M. Townley and James Winters did set in and upon one George Stevens and willfully, feloniously, deliberately and premeditatively and with malice aforethought, with force of arms, make an assault. . .with a certain revolving pistol then and there charged with gunpowder and leaden bullets. . .which they did discharge and shoot off, to, against, on, and through the said George Stevens, with the leaden bullets aforesaid, out of the revolving pistol aforesaid. . .and there unlawfully, feloniously, deliberately and premeditatedly, and with malice aforethought, did strike, penetrate, and kill said George Stevens."

Now that's a murder indictment.

October 27, 1983

Bohemian Cemetery Tells a Story

CAINSVILLE, Mo. -- The cemetery south of here sits on a hill above the Thompson River valley, land now stripped of drought-withered corn and soybeans or sown to winter wheat. With the recent rains, the wheat emerged, green shoots amid the rich, black soil.

The scene spread out below the cemetery is pure Missouriana--the fields, the greening wheat, even the hogs and the feeder cows on the farm just to the north.

Off to the northeast the silver Cainsville water tower gleams in the fall sun. The red and yellow and russet leaves on the changing trees almost hide the town. Fall, at least in rural Missouri, seems to have drawn itself out this year, giving more of what many feel is the best season.

No wonder the settlers all those years ago embraced the land, putting down roots and staying, birthing their children, rearing their families, even burying their dead in places like the little cemetery a half mile off Harrison County Route B where huge evergreens form a canopy over the tombstones.

The word settlers evokes an internal response. Weren't they probably Kentuckians or Ohioans or others-- you know, Americans--looking for new land in north Missouri? After all, isn't that who's buried in the little cemetery?

Not quite. The cemetery is not your typical Missouri burying ground.

Read a granite tombstone near the west edge of the cemetery, the lettering now murky from 101 years of weather. It goes:

Barbara Laba
Rozena Dankov
v. Lozgigh
22 Unora 1814
Zemrel
12 Rigna 1882

Tombstone after tombstone is like that, written in Bohemian, not an everyday language in north Missouri.

Christena Kolesh, the 81-year-old sexton of what is called the Bohemian Cemetery, moves forward to the stone and translates. The writing on the stone tells a short and simple story-- Barbora Laba, born Feb. 22, 1814, with the maiden name of Dankova in the city of Lozigigh in what is now Czechoslovakia, died July 12, 1882.

Mrs. Kolesh--her maiden name was Skakal, and she is one of the few people in what was a once-thriving pocket of Bohemian settlement who still speak and read the language-- moves to another stone. The letters cut in the granite are in English and Bohemian and give the name, age and dates of birth and death of a teenage boy who in the fall of 1913, quite simply, hanged himself.

Below the boy's name, a plaintive inscription is cut in the stone. It goes: *Ach! Muy milacku pojd domu mas branu oteurenou.* Under that are the English words--*Oh! My darling come home. The gate is open.*

"The boy's father was an American," says Mrs. Kokesh. "But his mother was a Bohemian, you know, used to the old ways."

According to Mrs. Kokesh's meticulously kept records, the cemetery holds 226 bodies and an urn with one man's cremated remains. Those beneath the ground are Bohemians, married to Bohemians, or the children of those unions. The preponderance of names are ones like Stoklasa, Ceradsky, Hrdlickova, Tomes and Mlika. But increasingly there are names like Young and Wilkinson and Huff. Many of the old names are fading away.

Mrs. Kokesh, who now lives over west at Ridgeway, Mo., but who for 40-odd years lived right next to the cemetery, isn't sure just why the Bohemians came to this particular spot in the late 1860s. (Josephine Prazak was the first burial, in 1869.) But they did, and soon Bohemian was as common as English on the streets and in the stores of Cainsville or in the once busy coal mine sunk on the south edge of town.

Some of the settlers farmed; others became cobblers and butchers and other sorts of tradesmen, making their way, admonishing their children to keep the old traditions. It was all right to learn English in school -- but speak Bohemian at home, they would say, and marry other Bohemians when that time comes.

And for 50 years the Bohemians marked their graves in the old country language, puzzling some of their non-Bohemian neighbors, starting a rumor that the Bohemians would get lonely for a loved one who'd died in the old country and put a stone with his or her name in the cemetery. Mrs. Kokesh scoffs at that, saying that there's somebody underneath every marker.

And the old Bohemians were sure that there would always be someone who could read the words saying they'd passed this way. But the language faded and, starting in the 1920s, it switched. "Born" was used for "rozena," and "died" for "zemrela."

"It's two miles to town," says Mrs. Kokesh. "And in the old, old days there used to be a horse-drawn hearse, all glass and black paint and black plumes on top, and it'd take ever so long to get here. And instead of flowers, like today, people would just take sprigs of evergreen and tie a ribbon on them, and that was plenty. Oh, I suppose that was something to see. I really do."

January 5, 1987

Giving Is His Life's Game Plan

TOPEKA--See that guy down the street? There, the one behind the trash truck, slinging metal cans full of refuse into the back.

Who's that? Why that's Grant Cushinberry, a semi-legend hereabouts. You say the name isn't familiar?

Ever hear of Andrew Carnegie or John D. Rockefeller? Or that skinny gent whose fortune started the Ford Foundation?

The word for those men was philanthropist. Well, ditto Grant Cushinberry.

More than ditto. When you figure out the proportion of Cushinberry's worth that he simply gives out of his own pocket to the people who need help, well, he makes Henry Ford and those others look like pikers.

Consider: for 20 years Cushinberry's been the linchpin of the annual Thanksgiving dinner for those without. The affair started small--maybe 200 people showing up at a local church.

This fall 5,500 people crowded into the Topeka city auditorium for turkey and fixings.

And Cushinberry's the one who has collected Christmas toys for children, seen that shut-ins got a meal and a visit on that day, and provided free Christmas trees for those who couldn't afford them.

He has organized and coached poor kids, hacked playing fields out of brush-covered vacant lots, taken what's called "Cushinberry's Kids" to the circus each winter, and grown vegetables on his corner lot called "God's Half Acre" and given them away. He has even established a free clothes pantry for those needing a warm coat.

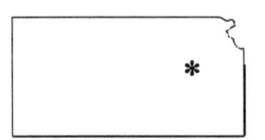

The list goes on. Mention "giving" here and it's a synonym for Grant Cushinberry: a proud 65-year-old farmer's son; a man who still has World War II shrapnel scars; the 1945 light-heavyweight champion of the Southwest Pacific; a college graduate; a psychiatric aide at institutions here for decades until his retirement; and now a trash hauler whose brightly painted truck's front bumper has the legend "Here Comes Cushinberry."

Indeed. Stories abound about Cushinberry putting the gentle but firm arm on businessmen and just ordinary folks to support various causes. Cushinberry, who lives here at 1919 Fillmore, can tell a story or two himself.

"At this year's turkey dinner here came Gov. Carlin," he says. "Naturally, I suggested a donation. He says, 'The state's broke.' And I said: 'You ain't.' And bless him, he gave me a $200 check."

Cushinberry's philosophy is simple. People don't need forms and bureaucracies, intimate questions and waiting in line in offices that erode their dignity. They need help.

So Grant Cushinberry, with his two pensions and his trash route, helps. He can't really tell you why--just that there are people out there who need a hand.

Some of that undoubtedly comes from his youth. He was born in Nicodemus, the tiny all-black community in western Kansas, and grew up in Hoisington. Being black in central Kansas five decades ago was no picnic. Cushinberry remembers scoring touchdowns in high school, then going to the victory celebration and being given orange drink in a paper cup while his teammates got theirs in a real glass. That was the way things were when you were black. No matter how talented you were.

But what he really remembers is that families helped each other with food and clothes and anything else. Not because they were black but because they were people in the same boat. You know, there but for the grace of God. . . .

That stuck.

"When you die what can you leave out there in the graveyard?" he asks. "Not money. Not stocks and bonds or property.

"All you can really leave is your good name."

Amen.

December 16, 1990

Murder Statistics Pale Next to Influenza Deaths

(KANSAS CITY, Mo.)--This being December, it's time to tote up statistics.

Death, for instance. Last week New York had achieved a dubious record: its 2,000th victim of violent death--murders mostly--since Jan. 1, 1990.

Those kinds of numbers are numbing. Two thousand? It seems inconceivable.

But go back 72 years. To 1918. Specifically to that year's December, the month after World War I ended, a time when the carmakers were announcing that their postwar vehicles would soon be in downtown Kansas City showrooms and when the front pages here were full of news about a streetcar strike.

Death?

Oh, it was around. Consider this paragraph from a story in *The Kansas City Star* on Dec. 6:

"The death rate at the [General] hospital remains at an alarming figure, 10 deaths occurring there yesterday. This is the largest number of deaths occurring at the hospital in any one day."

Or this, from *The Star*, Dec. 13:

"The vital statistics report yesterday includes 25 deaths."

What was happening in Kansas City? Murder? Buildings falling down? A string of trolley crashes?

The answer was in one terrible word: influenza.

Between September 1918, when the worldwide Spanish influenza pandemic reached Kansas City, and December 1918, when the sickness trailed off, 1,865 people died in Kansas City of influenza or resultant pneumonia. And that was in a far smaller Kansas City, one that didn't encompass 300-plus square miles, as it does today.

Thousands more died in Kansas and Missouri. The final death toll was in the hundreds of thousands in this country, millions around the world.

Yet to look back in old newspapers, one is struck not as much by the number of the deaths as by the coverage they received in the local newspapers.

The Star, in small, agate type, listed numbers--26 deaths on Dec. 3, 34 on Dec. 5, 57 on Dec. 10.

Headlines? Well, fitting with *The Star's* style, they were restrained, usually what was then called a "triple," a hard-to-write three-deck headline. Never more than a triple, though. Often the headlines would be even smaller, all but invisible under a two-deck headline.

Occasionally there would be a little feature story. Such as the one about William Davis, 35, an influenza sufferer who, half-naked and crazed with fever, led attendants at General Hospital on a 20-minute chase through the corridors. "Once he was restrained and taken back to his room he died," the story said matter-of-factly.

Inside the paper, in the death columns, one might see a line saying that so-and-so "died of influenza." But that was about it.

It was if some school district had an outbreak of head lice. Or that some employees were evacuated from a plant because of a chemical spill.

Why the subdued coverage?

Well, was it really subdued? People were told what was happening. But back then, long before radio and television, newspapers were the only outlet for news. They arbitrated what went where, what size headline went on the story, what importance the story received.

Today nearly 2,000 deaths in 120 days would result in screaming headlines, breathless newscasts, satellite feeds, and angry commentary.

Not in 1918. The flu and pneumonia were well-known killers.

It all came down to familiarity. And helplessness. And a certain fatalism. In 1918, people just died--carpenters and bankers, cleaning women and society ladies. Influenza, if anything, was a very democratic killer.

Now murder, at least in 1918, was different. It was front page news, no matter how senseless, how stupid.

Somehow, in the ensuing 72 years, it's all become reversed. Homicide and body counts have an almost easy familiarity now.

But an outbreak of a virulent disease that kills remorselessly? Now that would be different.

That would be news.

October 6, 1983

Bad Seeds Also Grew on Prairie

HALSTEAD, Kan. -- Judging from contemporary accounts, Nellie Bailey, *nee* Benthusen, was quite a looker.

Still, the prose of a century ago loses something. Nellie, a Halstead girl, was described as "of fine figure, delicate, sylphlike of movement, with strongly arched eyebrows and thin lips."

One can't argue with the description of Nellie's lips and eyebrows--they were thin (lips) and bushy (eyebrows). But pictures of her, published in her 1885 autobiography, show a woman who looked a little like a middle linebacker.

All that didn't matter Jan. 15, 1885, a time when women were in short supply in Kansas. Nellie, dressed to the nines, entered the Wichita Opera House, where 2,000 wild-eyed people had turned up for Nellie's trial on a charge of murdering Clement Bothamley, an English stockman, dope addict, bigamist and arthritic. The late Mr. Bothamley had expired on the prairie in the Oklahoma Territory in early October 1883. Nellie had been present at the time.

Authorities in Wichita said they had to use the opera house for the trial. It was the only place that could hold everybody.

At the time of the trial, Nellie was all of 22 years old. But of course, she wasn't like a lot of women her age in Kansas. No hauling buffalo chips for Nellie; no plugging the rat holes in the soddy; no delivering her first child by herself. Nellie was not a pioneer. But undoubtedly she was the closest this state ever got to a *femme fatale*. The crowds that flooded the opera house attested to that.

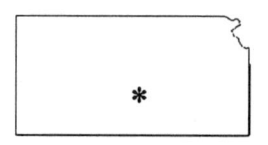

From what investigators could learn about Nellie before the trial -- an outfit named the British-American Association of Kansas was hot for her conviction since the deceased was a member -- Nellie had led a fairly normal childhood. There were little things: Nellie's brother was a thief, Nellie was a kleptomaniac herself, and there was some evidence that Nellie's father had conspired with the hired girl to poison Nellie's mother with a dollop of strychnine that would have dropped a brace of mules.

Nellie's mother, however, took the poison, told the hired girl she was an incompetent nurse, recovered and "lived in at least fair harmony with her husband for many years."

So there was some instability. At 18 Nellie came within eight days of marrying a very nice Illinois youth but threw him over for a very rich (and much older) Kansas banker named Shannon Bailey. There was a problem. Nellie was flirtatious, often being ejected from hotels for "flagrant" conduct. Then as now, "flagrant" didn't mean stealing towels.

Mr. Bailey lasted two years, traveling all over the country with Nellie and finally, according to Nellie, giving her $4,000 before retiring into the interior of Canada, never to be seen again.

With her money, Nellie went to Kansas City to become an actress. She apparently married a man named Reese in Wisconsin who later testified that he lived in a state of adultery with Nellie for some months but never consummated the marriage. Mr. Reese did not clarify that statement.

Eventually Nellie returned to Kansas, ran into Mr. Bothamley and agreed to live with him if they could move away from Halstead. Nellie, despite a checkered couple of years -- she was also suspected of murder in Oregon -- said she did not want to scandalize Halstead or her parents, who were living in relative bliss. Willie, Nellie's brother, was by then in the penitentiary.

Mr. Bothamley, in the United States only a few years, was no prize. But he had money and land. He had deserted his wife and two children in England despite being a descendant of the Duke of Marlborough. His arthritis was so bad that his favorite pastime of visiting gunsmiths invariably meant several guns went off when he stumbled against or poked at the merchandise. He also drank and took daily morphine injections.

At the trial the prosecution claimed Nellie had murdered Mr. Bothamley for his land and money. He had signed the deeds over to her.

The defense explained that Mr. Bothamley had managed to stretch his arthritic arms several feet behind him, turned the pistol upside down and, despite being drugged, then shot himself in the back of the head with unerring accuracy.

After five minutes of deliberation, the jurors, many of them weeping, acquitted Nellie. She left the opera house "the bravest little woman in Kansas," as one newspaper rhapsodized, and headed for the nearest ghostwriter.

Within months her autobiography (*The Life of Nellie C. Bailey*) was out, the last 100 pages being devoted to her ancestors' singular role in winning the Revolutionary War.

February 6, 1987

A Brand Name for Posterity

JEFFERSON CITY -- Somehow you get the idea that C.D. Gregg wasn't playing with a full deck when, in 1911, he fielded a trademark application with the secretary of state's office here.

Gregg, who was in the beverage business over in St. Louis, wanted to market tea, coffee, and soft drinks. In the early part of this century, that was a big deal because anybody could see the success Coca-Cola and Lipton's were having.

Because of an 1893 Missouri law, Gregg needed a trademark. He came up with a doozy.

His application asked--are you ready for this?--for the exclusive use of the word Booze.

You know, Booze tea. Or Booze pop. Looking back, it's apparent Gregg was somewhat out of touch with reality in those pre-prohibitionary times. And it's pretty obvious his beverages never really caught the public fancy. Elsewise we'd have had a cup of Booze coffee this morning.

This all comes to mind because of a delightful exhibit at the Missouri Archives here showing the artistic diversity of the various trademarks that have arrived here over the years.

The law required a sample of the trademark. What happened was that most people didn't send a drawing. They just ripped a label off a bottle of liquor, mashed up an empty carton of crackers or sent a flour sack along. Things were pretty informal in those days.

The diversity is apparent, but what's really charming is the straightforward approach taken by those designing a label or a logo to attract buyers.

Exhibited on the lobby wall is the self-explanatory Death O'Fly poison trademarked in 1911 by a St. Joseph firm; Gladiator axle grease, an 1897 St. Louis product; and the American Lady bread that started selling around Jefferson City in 1937.

There was nothing slick about the labels, not like today. Prestone antifreeze showed a car radiator and a thermometer; Cinderella flour pictured the prince fitting a shoe on guess who; and Anti-Trust rye whiskey showed Lady Liberty wrapped in an American flag.

And the names. There are some 60,000 of them, all filed by folks who probably thought their products were sure bets.

It was a simpler time, one long before a company like Esso would spend millions to come up with a Madison Avenue name like Exxon, or before the old Pacific Bell would create a jawbreaker name like Pacific Telesis.

How about Bad Debt Collector wearing apparel, a St. Louis brand? Didn't the guy dunning you always wear better clothes than yours?

Or You Chu chewing gum? Tabasco underwear? Perfection Pile Cure?

Or try this for the actual name of a brand of pants--$1.75 A Leg, 2 Legs For $3.50.

Nor were imports a big deal. You cold be pretty sure of where you were buying from with names like Ozark brand pants; Mizzoo refrigerators, or Pride of Kansas City cigars.

Naturally, there were the names we still recognized: B.V.D.'s, Lysol, Bit-O-Honey.

And near-misses. Elbert Nichols, a St. Louis man who'd come up with a cattle dehorning paste, called it Noxem. If he'd have added an "a" he's have probably become a face cleansing mogul.

Still, the old-timers occasionally showed a flair that would make the ad boys of today weep. Take F.S. Weaver of St. Joseph, who knew his newly designed egg carton really wasn't that much different from anybody else's. What could he do? How about promoting freshness through a name?

Weaver did. He called his egg carton the Yesterlaid carton.

Perfect.

October 24, 1984

Town Left Its Mark on History

TORONTO, Kan. -- Greenwood City was three miles north of here until the early 1870s, when it gasped and died after landowners found that their deeds were worthless, the actual ownership of the town resting in the hands of a 7-year-old boy.

That story alone, too involved to repeat here, makes Greenwood City unique. Yet being owned by a stripling was only a minor chapter in the short, flamboyant passage of this town of 900 toward oblivion.

This all came to mind this week with Kansas City wallowing in self-congratulations after the presidential debate. Kansas City often seems to forget that it has a past, too. A century ago garden brunches and champagne parties for visiting reporters and politicians weren't really too common in a town that came within an eyelash of carrying the name Toad-a-Loop, Mo., into the 20th century. Toad-a-Loop was a corruption of the French Tour-de-Loup or Wolf Run, which the local yahoos apparently found impossible to pronounce.

Somehow, one has the impression that Toad-a-Loop, Mo., would not have been picked as a presidential debate site. Maybe, if it had survived, Greenwood City would have become a bustling city and, who knows, been in the running for a joint appearance by President Reagan and Walter F. Mondale.

If it had, residents of Greenwood City could have pointed out their colorful history to visiting 1984 journalists.

Greenwood City, you see, was sort of different as far as Kansas cow towns went. Oh, there was a brewery and a distillery. But only a rare "soiled dove" entered the city limits. Why has never been determined, except that perhaps the copious supplies of ethyl alcohol had a desensitizing effect on the cowboys, who, in all other respects, acted like cowboys, regularly getting drunk and shooting up the place.

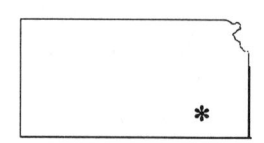

"For noise and boisterous rowdyism, Greenwood City was in the front rank of frontier towns," one chronicler wrote proudly.

Many of the cowboys were on enforced vacations in Kansas, being loath to return to a strand of Texas hemp. They included Kinch West, Jack Tedford, Bill Holliman, Vid Farr and a man who went by the marvelous moniker of William the Innocent.

Mr. Holliman, however, apparently had moments of introspection, and one day he approached Edgar Walters, a town resident, and asked whether there was a Sunday school in the area.

"Why don't you start one here in Greenwood City?" Mr. Holliman asked. Mr. Walters said he feared the cowboys would shoot up any Sunday school.

"Not much we wouldn't," Mr. Holliman replied. "I've talked it over with the boys. They think it's too damn bad there hain't no place to go on Sunday. You start it and I'll come and Kinch West will come. We'll shoot the first man that misbehaves."

Mr. Walters thought it might be more respectful to keep guns out of church. Mr. Holliman said no, some marshal might get the drop on "the boys."

"And let's have it in the forenoon," Mr. Holliman said. "The boys will want to git drunk in the afternoon."

The Sunday school was started. It survived several years, even after Greenwood City and the cowboys were only a memory.

There are a couple of other stories about the town. One of the natives was Wayne Brazel, who in 1906 killed Pat Garrett near Las Cruces, N.M. Mr. Garrett was the man who killed Billy the Kid, a New Yorker who had lived briefly in southeast Kansas.

And then there was John P. Mitchell, a land speculator and the town's founder, who inadvertently allowed title of the town to pass to a child.

Naturally, this caused some bitterness. Over two decades, while in and out of disputing the land titles in the courts, Mr. Mitchell became a target for men with large-caliber guns who thought the courts lacked alacrity.

"He was never the shooter," one man recalled. "But what he might be called is a 'professional shootee.' More men shot at him than any man I ever knew in civil life. And the strange thing was he never sought revenge. In fact, he never had a harsh word for anybody."

Apparently, through luck and errant aim, Mr. Mitchell died in bed, a failed man in terms of town founding but an eminently successful one in dodging bullets.

September 23, 1990

Civil War Raged Out Here Too with Incredible Savagery

(KANSAS CITY, Mo.)--Publicity for "The Civil War," a PBS documentary that begins tonight, contains this sentence:

"The documentary vividly embraces the entire sweep of the war."

Well, not quite. The 11-hour series largely omits what happened on what then was part of the western frontier--Kansas and Missouri.

The series concentrates on the war east of the Mississippi River, understandable since that is where Lee and Grant fought great battles; where Lincoln and Davis approved momentous decisions.

Moreover, it was where the practitioners of the new profession of photography (indispensable for a 1990 television show) plied their craft; where illustrators illustrated; where newspaper correspondents wrote reams of copy that later became the basis of history books.

Back then, the frontier, and more precisely where this will be read this morning, was a backwater, a place of mud roads and rude trails; one where the westward dreamers and dispossessed paused briefly; a region of scant industry and thrown-together shacks, few newspapers and even fewer telegraph wires. There was only the rare photographer, one who mostly took tintypes of stern-visaged men and worn women.

This was the "West," a hard land, far from congressional rancor and philosophical drawing room debate about man's condition in relation to his government. Fort Sumter was far away.

Thus tonight, thousands in Missouri and Kansas and millions elsewhere will watch what critics are calling a fine documentary, looking, in a sense, eastward. And mostly unaware of these things:

· The Civil War could be said to have begun out here, specifically six years before Fort Sumter when an anti-abolitionist named G.W. Clarke "cleaned out" Linn and Miami counties in Kansas, driving off settlers, scattering their livestock, burning their cabins.

· Violence, a simmering constant under the rough patina of the frontier, erupted again when Missourians sacked Lawrence. Then the crazed eyes of John Brown watched as pro-slavery men (including two teenagers) were butchered on the Marais des Cygnes. Tit for tat. There was no debate and little subtlety -- what was at stake in Missouri was $35 million worth of slaves. In Kansas were the rich, newly opened farmlands. Slavery and abolition got lip service. And the sanguinary excess became a whirlwind. In 1861, declared war was an easy step.

- The first major battle of the Civil war was at Carthage, Mo., two weeks before First Bull Run.
- The first use of black combat troops was in Bates County, Mo.
- There were plenty of battles -- Lexington, Boonville, First and Second Newtonia, Mine Creek, Lone Jack, Wilson's Creek, Pilot Knob and Westport, all small compared with an Antietam or Gettysburg, but still ones in which poised lines of soldiers disintegrated before flame-tipped musketry.
- Guerrilla warfare, rivaling that of Vietnam, eventually defined the war here. There were murders. And hangings. And torture.

It was a grinding savagery that even now is almost beyond belief -- men taking other men's ears and hanging them, as if garlands, from their horses' reins; men tied in hog lots and left for pigs to eat; women raped; civilians scalped; prisoners shot out of hand; mutinies; riots; even starvation in what were essentially concentration camps.

All in Missouri and Kansas.

And soldiers were sent to small towns with orders to kill people. No trial, no court martial. Just this, issued from Fort Scott, Kan., October 6, 1862:

"You will. . .send a discreet party of three or four dressed in citizens clothes. . .to Burlington [Kan.] to. . . kill one desperado engaged in molesting the families of soldiers. Report to Osere Kent and be governed by his suggestions."

No one was safe. Fear was a knock on the door. The whole tier of counties south of Kansas City became a wasteland. Jasper County, Mo., dropped in population from 7,000 to 200; Carthage from 600 to five. Travelers in 1866 recalled not fields or crops or yeoman farmers, only blackened chimneys against the sky.

The legacy was gall, but also ennobling myth. Yet not the bloodless ones such as would rise in the Eastern states. In Missouri, the James boys, the Youngers, the other cutthroats, became part of "The Lost Cause" of the Confederacy.

Likewise, in Kansas, old men would remember Jennison, Montgomery and Lane, cutthroats too.

Until well into this century, they didn't forget. Some haven't yet.

A church in southern Missouri would refuse to have south-facing windows became it never wanted the "traitorous winds of the Confederacy" to despoil its interior.

Just a year ago a monument to "Bloody Bill" Anderson, a killer, not a soldier, was erected near Orrick, Mo.

Enjoy the television series. But tomorrow, look around. What happened on the screen happened here. In spades.

August 23, 1983

'H' Marked the Roads in Kansas

PHILLIPSBURG, Kan. -- The heavy-gauge metal sign, red-lettered "H-H," was found west of Stuttgart, Kan., last month. It was a curiosity. Eventually a picture of it appeared in the *Phillips County Review,* McDill "Huck" Boyd's paper.

In his weekly column Mr. Boyd asked readers whether anybody remembered the H-H highway. Nobody did.

"We haven't got a clue," said Mr. Boyd, who added that lots of folks here did remember the old "Pikes Peak, Ocean to Ocean Highway," the forerunner of U.S. 36. People recalled that that highway was marked with red and white bands nailed on telephone and telegraph poles and that it made a lot of turns, making sure it hit every little town, following the section lines from town to town across Kansas.

But nobody remembered any highway marked with a big red "H."

"Oh, that's easy," said Bob Knecht, curator of maps for the Kansas Historical Society in Topeka, after looking at the picture that ran in the paper. "That's a Hockaday route, marked with the first letter of his name. There's two 'H's on it because it's telling the motorist to go straight ahead. If there'd been a left or right turn, there'd just have been a single 'H' on it and a big arrow giving the direction."

What was found near Stuttgart, then, wasn't just a piece of bullet-riddled metal; it was a piece of Kansas history. More specifically it was a tangible reminder of a man named F. W. "Woody" Hockaday, a Wichita auto supply dealer, the man who bought the first train ticket ever at Kansas City's Union Station and, later, an eccentric. Starting in 1913 and continuing into the 1920s he spent $100,000 of his own money marking 60,000 miles of roads in Kansas, Oklahoma and North Texas.

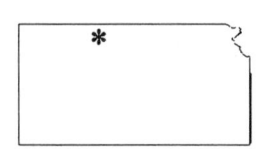

In the process Mr. Hockaday went broke. By the time the state tardily assumed responsibility for marking roads, he'd turned to having people write the names of nearby towns on their barn roofs so that aviators could find their way. Indeed that was the beginning of the nation's air lanes.

But as the years passed, Mr. Hockaday acted stranger and stranger, was committed to several private sanitariums and public institutions and was declared insane in 1938 after unsuccessfully trying to jump into President Roosevelt's car in Oklahoma City to, as he said, "shine FDR's shoes."

He then became an anti-war advocate before it was popular, going around the country to American Legion meetings just before and during World War II, ripping open pillows and yelling that "feathers are better than bullets any day."

No one denied that Mr. Hockaday was unique. Letters to newspapers back in the '30s and '40s expressed sorrow over his deteriorating mental condition. The letters were even sadder when the slight, bespectacled man (whom the police invariably beat to within an inch of his life when they arrested him) died in a private sanitarium in Macon, Mo., in 1947 at age 63.

Yet his impact had been singular, especially on Kansas roads. Although it quickly faded there was talk in 1954 of naming the new Kansas Turnpike after him.

Originally Mr. Hockaday put out his "H" signs as an advertising gimmick. Backtracking from any "H" sign, placed for easy visibility alongside the road, would bring a motorist in his Model T or Marmon back to mile zero on the Hockaday road network, namely his Wichita auto supply store.

Mile zero for the nation's road network, between 1913 and the 1920s, was Wichita, not Washington as it is now. All roads led to Wichita. Mr. Hockaday's business prospered. People driving back then, literally from section line to sectional line, were known to bless Mr. Hockaday's name when the "H" signs appeared. And they weren't on poles; they were beside the road for easier viewing. Quite simply: people that Mr. Hockaday saved from spending a night on some deserted Kansas section line road made loyal customers.

By 1918, Mr. Hockaday even was issuing red and white maps, calling his system the Hockaday National Roads, advising drivers what was paved (very little), what was dirt (most everything else) and what was to be avoided at all costs.

Yet the advertising gimmick apparently gave way to a crusade. More and more Mr. Hockaday was absent from his business, and it declined rapidly. He was out on some back road putting up signs, figuring out which routes were best for travelers. Mr. Hockaday not only marked roads -- he built at least one south of Sterling, Kan. And he named them. Kansas 96 has that number because that was Mr. Hockaday's business telephone number.

Quite simply, Mr. Hockaday showed the way to a generation of motorists, a man now largely forgotten except for a battered red and white metal sign found near Stuttgart, Kan.

July 18, 1981

Race May Put Town on the Map

OMAHA, Mo., -- "This town is definitely growing," says Bob McCollom, his voice taking on a tinge of unabashed boosterism. He tongue was in his cheek.

"When the town was founded in 1863 it had seven people. Now we've got 11. You know what that is? By God, that's a 58 percent increase over 118 years!"

McCollom, 56, a combat Marine in the Pacific and a big-city advertising account executive for 30 years before coming back to run the family owned Omaha General Store in 1979, is obviously bullish on this north Missouri hamlet. Others have been less charitable.

Several years ago the Missouri highway commission excised Omaha from the official state road map and, in effect, caused the cluster of homes and buildings at the junction of Missouri 149 and Putnam County Route Z to disappear.

That may change at 2 p.m. Sunday when entrants in the First Annual Great Omaha to the Iowa Line and Back Mule and Horse Race break from the starting line on Route Z, head for nearby Livonia, Mo., for a quarter mile, cut north on a dirt road called the Chariton cutoff, and race to the Iowa line and back.

"It's a total of 4.8 miles one way," says McCollom. "So that means 9.6 miles from here to Iowa and back. The first quarter-mile is on blacktop, the rest dirt. There's a $10 entry fee, winner take all. All that money will be in a coffee can at the finish line for the winner."

McCollom doesn't know how many entries to expect. He's had calls about the race from all over Missouri, and Iowa and Illinois. Two weeks ago, the original date for the race, about 100 people and five riders gather despite heavy rains that had washed out the Coon Creek bridge and left the Chariton cutoff a muddy trace.

"People knew the race might be postponed, so I don't think those five riders were representative of how many we can expect," says McCollom.

The only sure entry, McCollom says, is James Leach and his big mule, Cotton, both from nearby Livonia. McCollom says Leach, a big, raw-boned man in his 30s, is convinced he and Cotton can win.

McCollom says Leach looks a little bit like Cotton. Or maybe it's that Cotton looks a little bit like Leach.

"They're a pair, all right," McCollom says. "Old Jim hates that mule with a passion, and that mule hates old Jim. They're always trying to kill each other. They're perfect for each other. The other day Jim and Cotton were practicing, and they headed down Z toward the cutoff road. 'Cept Cotton, when he got to the cutoff, kept going straight. It was a sight to see. And to hear Jim cuss that mule."

McCollom hopes the race will put Omaha back on the map, literally. He figures some Jefferson City bureaucrat arbitrarily decided Omaha should be left off the map, or some third-level paste-up artist dropped the type for Omaha on the floor and was too lazy to pick it up.

"Seriously," he says, "everybody says we've got to maintain the small rural communities. But then they take us off the map. When I came back here I wrote the highway department. They wrote they wanted only incorporated towns with a real city government on the map. Well, isn't that nice! What business do they have to tell us to incorporate or to have a mayor and council? We do pretty good. We've just started a fire department, a darn good one, and we didn't need the state for that."

McCollom says the highway department stopped replying to his letters when he threatened to file a $6 million class-action lawsuit against the state on behalf of the residents because Omaha's name was dropped off the map. The amount of the lawsuit, he says, seemed like a nice round figure.

"I had grounds," he says. "All those years I'd tell people that I was from Omaha, Mo., but there was no Omaha, Mo., on the map., Call it anguish. Call it pain and suffering and embarrassment before my peers in Indianapolis, Chicago, Kansas City, New York and Milwaukee. They thought Omaha was where the Union Pacific is -- in Nebraska. A jury, you know, just might see my side."

If the mule and horse race doesn't do it, McCollom has other plans. He may publish his own map and leave Jefferson City off it. And there's always the possibility of incorporation, running the city limits four miles north and asking Iowa if Omaha can be on its road map.

"We've only just started," McCollom says.

August 8, 1984

Hats Off to an Early Bohemian

LAWRENCE, Kan. -- This is Harry Hibbard Kemp's centennial year.

Well, more or less. It's nice to be exact, especially on centennials for former University of Kansas students. When Mr. Kemp died in 1960 his age was given as 76. So that'd make him 100 this year.

But in his autobiography -- Mr. Kemp wasn't short on humility and wrote his life story when he was only 38 -- he said that he was born in the early or mid-1880's. So it was probably 1884.

Now some people may be wondering just who Harry Hibbard Kemp was. Well, the 1920s labeled him a "literary light," a phrase that fortunately isn't heard much anymore. He was the "Tramp Poet" of America, the bard of the boxcars. He was a young man who bummed here in 1906 with "enough hair on his head for six poets." Plus sandals. Mr. Kemp enrolled, majoring in German, Latin, Greek, philosophy and literature, and, at least until the weather turned cold, living naked on an island in the middle of the Kaw River.

In short, Mr. Kemp was probably the first hippie to land in Lawrence.

He wasn't the last.

Yet Mr. Kemp, who'd ridden the rails for years and scribbled poetry on his meanderings, did something on his arrival that has probably been done only a few times since, especially since some classes are now only slightly smaller than the buffalo herds that once ranged the state. He talked a professor into paying his fees. Then he went back to his sunbathing.

That singular feat caught the attention of other students. But there were other things. Male students in those days of late summer in Kansas wore stiff Celluloid collars and straw boaters. Mr. Kemp wore no hat, a sartorial omission that brought a reporter around for an interview. News was not known for its depth then, and the article, subsequently appearing in other papers, led with Mr. Kemp's hatless attire and then went into his approbation of anarchy, syndicalism and socialism. It added that Mr. Kemp had the unheard-of gall to argue with his professors right in class.

Mr. Kemp explained that not wearing a hat was part of his physical culture regimen. Mr. Kemp, besides living naked, was strong on good muscle tone.

Still, it was little wonder that there was interest in Mr. Kemp. There were assorted crazies running around Kansas in those days--and the newspapers, largely Republican, were always vigilant for newcomers to the asylum.

Mr. Kemp was a modern man in one sense. He knew how to massage the press. Within a few months he was a regular guest in William Allen White's Emporia home and a friend of Ida Tarbell, the muckraker. His clipping file grew apace. Occasionally he was even getting five bucks from a magazine for a poem.

After graduating from KU in 1908, Mr. Kemp headed east. He had cut his hair and embraced writer Upton Sinclair's ideas on free love. There is strong indication he was also soon embracing Mr. Sinclair's wife, Meta, since the two ran off together, Meta leaving when Mr. Kemp announced that daily employment wasn't his metier.

Mr. Kemp came to roost in Greenwich Village, sort of founding the place for bohemians. He described himself as an actor-poet-playwright, and he married. Twice. He sold many of his poems to *The New York Times*, a sure indication his radicalism had mellowed.

In 1922 his autobiography appeared and went through three quick reprintings. It was pretty racy. Publisher White thought it should have been awarded the Pulitzer Prize, an odd lapse for him, because *Tramping Through Life* was full of sentences such as, "My gaze grew fat with the pleasure of her nakedness." A Topeka paper called Mr. Kemp's work "repulsive and erotic," an endorsement that obviously boosted sales in Kansas.

Mr. Kemp's poetry was about the same, describing Kansas as a place with "green armies of corn" and where "miles of wheat ripple beneath the wind's light feet."

In his later years Mr. Kemp settled in Provincetown, Mass., at the tip of Cape Cod, founded a theater company and narrowed his vision as all of us do with age. His last effort was to debunk Plymouth Rock, saying history was wrong and surely the Pilgrims landed first across the bay at Provincetown.

November 14, 1981

He Nails down a Bit of History

SCHELL CITY, Mo. -- Gordon Hanna felt his way along, his right hand touching the hammers hung above his head.

"Let's see," he said.. "I'm looking for one with a chip out of the face. When I feel it, I'll have the right one. Oh, here it is."

With that, Mr. Hanna slipped a massive ball peen hammer off a nail and held it out. True enough, the face was chipped. The word "COPE" was stamped on the side in capital letters.

"A Mr. Cope down south of here gave me this hammer," Mr. Hanna recalled. "Next day he up and died. That's happened more than once-- somebody giving me a hammer and then in a day or so just passing on."

Mortality and hammers wouldn't seem to mix, but they do in Mr. Hanna's case. More than one dying man around here has had his will drawn and relatives poised for the funeral and still made sure Mr. Hanna got his hammer.

"A hammer is personal," said Mr. Hanna, who is a spry 86. "A man may have worked with a certain hammer all his life. So he doesn't want it thrown in the corner and forgotten. So he gives it to me and I hang it in my shed."

Mr. Hanna's shed is a backyard museum of hammers. Exactly 223 hammers are hung from the ceiling. All are different. There are carpenters' hammers and metal-working hammers, blacksmiths' hammers, hammers to shape guttering and coopers' hammers, hammers for making horseshoes, and even a slaughterhouse killing hammer.

The odd thing, said Mr. Hanna, is that although the hammer assumed its basic form centuries ago, the tool has been malleable to various shapes for specific jobs. A screwdriver is just a screwdriver, basically changeable only in size. Not a hammer.

"Now look at this hammer," Mr. Hanna said. "Look at the length of the tang here on the rear. See, it's not split like one on a claw hammer. Now what's that long tang used for? Simple. It was used to hammer hoops down on barrel staves."

Mr. Hanna took another hammer, which looked like a regular claw hammer but had an opening the shape of a "T" on the tang just above the claw. Two ball bearings were inside the "T." Mr. Hanna clamped the hammer between his legs, inserted a nail head first into the "T" with his right hand, grabbed the hammer with the same hand, and swung it backward to start the nail.

One the nail was started, Mr. Hanna jerked the hammer upward, the spring-loaded ball bearings released the nail, and Mr. Hanna turned the hammer over and pounded the nail in the wood.

"This is nothing more than a hammer for a man with one arm," he said, smiling. "I show this to the young people who come in here. They can't believe people years ago were smart enough to figure out something like this."

Mr. Hanna said he's enjoyed showing children his hammers. Most of them think a hammer is what they see hanging in a supermarket's home utensils section. They don't realize, he said, that hammers, in a very real way, shaped this country--shoeing the horses, building the railroads, killing the hogs and steers, and even supporting a few carpenters with one hand.

And hammers have been important in Mr. Hanna's life. He started as a machinist in northwest Missouri in 1909 at 14. His first job was to make a hammer.

"The boss figured if you couldn't make a hammer, well you weren't a machinist," said Mr. Hanna. "I made my hammer--in fact, I've still got it-- and by the time I was 17, I was the lead machinist."

Mr. Hanna made a living as a machinist. A man who can cut and shape metal can always make a living, he said. He married--he and Betha Hanna recently celebrated their 51st wedding anniversary--and there was a daughter, Mary, now married herself. He and Mrs. Hanna retired in 1961 and started counting their grandchildren and great-grandchildren. And Mr. Hanna started collecting his hammers. As his collection grew, people started giving him hammers.

"And I go to flea markets and sales," he said. "I got these two from the rubble at the old fort at Fort Scott. And I've got some that go back to the 1700s. See, they don't look a whole lot different."

Although Mr. Hanna has been offered several thousand dollars for his hammers, he isn't selling. Still, he doesn't kid himself about his own mortality. He may donate the collection.

"I think it ought to be in one piece," he said. "It's part of what's happened over the past couple of hundreds years. Now so much is just plastic. And it won't last. Not like a hammer."

April 5, 1978

Twin Twisters: Impossibly Possible

The darkness became intense with fearful rapidity, sending terror into the hearts of the bravest. People were trying to collect their wits and accustom themselves to the great calamity already befallen them, but on the advent of this second monster all hope fled and the wildest terror reigned supreme.

Many thought the millennium was surely at hand.

(KANSAS CITY, Mo.)--It's tornado season, at least the start of it, and the lines above are taken from a worn old volume called "Professional Papers of the Signal Service, Volume IV," which Allen Pearson, director of the National Severe Storms Forecast Center, keeps in his office in Kansas City.

The volume was published in 1881; the binding is cracked but the book is a treasure for Pearson, who keeps at his fingertips a variety of odd facts and figures about his business--forecasting tornados.

Pearson can tell you about the "tri-state tornado" of 1925 that killed 600 persons; the tornado in the late 1890s that demolished most of St. Louis, and a variety of other tornado-related facts.

And he can show you the old volume, an official U.S. government document, which tells of the day 99 years ago that the small town of Irving, near Blue Rapids in north central Kansas, became a legend among tornado forecasters.

Irving, population 300, was the great exception in all tornado forecasting--on May 30, 1879, it was hit by two tornados in one day.

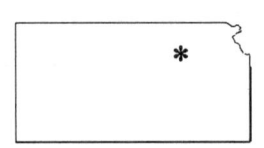

"Things like that just aren't supposed to happen," says Pearson. "But that day, in that place, they did."

Irving doesn't exist any more. It was swallowed up by the waters that made Tuttle Creek Reservoir in the 1960s.

But in May 1879 it was a prosperous little town, full of new settlers who had moved to Kansas hoping to make a go of it on the surrounding prairies. Many were Germans.

Irving was hard by the Big Blue River, a new stone-and-iron bridge had just been completed, and there were two banks and several churches in town--sure signs that the future was assured. About the only problem was the dry spring: there was some concern over the crops.

May 30 broke dry and clear but toward the middle of the afternoon the weather turned sultry and hot. Several townspeople noted the steady wind blowing out of the southwest.

By 4 p.m., unbeknownst to the residents of Irving, tornados had formed to the southwest in Riley County. Residents there said the storms came up quickly, turning the sky black in the southwest and northwest. Within minutes, huge masses of black clouds mingled with lighter ones and the first funnels were on the ground, destroying the corn cribs and stables of a settler named Naninaga near Walnut Creek.

There were, in fact, two funnel clouds, one large, the other smaller, which had dropped from the clouds. They wrecked everything in their path--barns, stables, houses, trees.

The funnels took off toward Irving but no alarm was sounded.

Tornados were little understood in those days. Any forecast of such phenomena was made in Washington anyway and most likely would have been sent by train. The U.S. Army Signal Service, forerunner of the weather bureau, just made the forecasts to be making forecasts--they didn't bother telegraphing them to affected areas.

The funnels joined as one near the tiny community of Randolph, Kan., where residents watched the storm's progress to the west of town with a mixture of fear and awe. Some said it "sounded like a thousand railroad trains."

The funnel blew down a schoolhouse shortly after students had been dismissed, tore up the woods along the bottoms of North Otter Creek, then swung west, where it struck the home of Adam Schwein, killing an infant but sparing the mother, a Mrs. Schwein, who was holding the child.

By this time the funnel was in Marshall County and nearing Irving. Another schoolhouse was demolished, then a group of houses. One belonged to a man named Robert Reed, who said later that the funnel lifted his home "as easily as a feather."

Reed decided to escape, ran out the door--and fell 30 or so feet to the ground, injuring himself severely. Two other homes were demolished, killing two persons.

Now Irving was only a mile distant. The funnel, still on the ground, passed over another creek, demolished a house, killing a woman and her four children. Their bodies were found, as the government report said, "perfectly devoid of clothing."

Then the funnel described as "like an elephant's trunk," was in Irving.

Six died at the Gale residence, their clothing torn to shreds and stripped from their bodies. Five more were injured at the Gallop house, which was lifted off the ground and set back down with its stone chimney still intact.

A wagon carrying a thousand board-feet of lumber disappeared without a trace, barbed wire was twisted like rope and tethered livestock was left with every bone broken.

Finally the tornado was past Irving in the bottoms along the Big Blue. As a malicious afterthought, the funnel turned north up the river to demolish the 130-foot bridge, which until that moment had been the pride of all Marshall County.

Then it was over. The tornado disappeared to the northeast and the empty prairies. Residents came out of their cellars and storm shelters, feeling the rain beat on their faces and seeing the sun come out along the western horizon. A cold wind sprang up out of the northwest.

"Hardly had the people recovered from the first shock," said the government report, "when there appeared in the west a cloud of inky blackness and enormous dimensions."

The residents were thunderstruck. Several started shrieking and moaning, their cries joining with those injured by the first tornado.

To no avail.

The second storm roared into Irving from the west (the first had been from the west-southwest), flattening what was left. Eighteen houses clustered together were smashed immediately, then nine others, and then five more, including two churches and the grain elevator. Almost 50 buildings were demolished this time--meaning most of the town.

And the storm passed, disappearing like the first onto the empty prairies.

Oddly, only five died in the second tornado. One, a Mrs. Keeney, was found sticking straight up out of the mud near her home, her head and shoulders buried in the earth. And ironically, there was another mother holding her child. This time the mother died, but the infant survived.

In all, 19 died. Scores were injured. Irving was rubble, and that wasn't all, the government report continued: "The effect upon the people was pitiful. Night after night hundreds of people never went to bed, but remained dressed and with their lanterns trimmed, watching for a fresh onslaught, which they expected momentarily. Every dark cloud seemed to them filled with forebodings, which could not be allayed until every vestige of the supposed danger had vanished.

"The terror was something beyond description."

Barn Billboards--One Part Nostalgia, One Part Ad Blitz

(KANSAS CITY, Mo.)--The demise of Burma Shave a couple months ago meant the sure end of those roadside ditties that entertained a generation of two of American motorists. But Hark! All is not lost for the reading driver. There are still those painted barns featuring the Meramec Caverns, Rock City (in some parts of the country) and Mail Pouch Chewing Tobacco.

You know Mail Pouch. It's advertised in those tremendous white-and-yellow letters on the sides and ends of barns. Unlike Burma Shave's small road signs, the Mail Pouch ads are still going strong, being painted and renewed even to this day by one Harley Warrwick, whose stomping grounds are Ohio, West Virginia, and Pennsylvania.

In our part of the country, though, what you see is all you'll ever get. According to Stuart F. Bloch, a vice president of General Cigar & Tobacco Co., Wheeling, W. Va., the company stopped painting barns in Missouri, Kansas, Arkansas, and Oklahoma decades ago.

There probably are still some left in the region and the federal government is even protecting them and other such examples of early advertising art "as part of the American folk heritage." (Bloch, and, in fact, *The Kansas City Times* would like to know of any in the region, so if you see one, write us.)

The current barns are no problem. Bloch can tell you where they are because they're kept on a computer list. There are several hundred of them, mostly in the area where Ohio, West Virginia and Pennsylvania come together.

Bloch makes a simple point:

"In American advertising, three outfits have developed their own medium--meaning they haven't depended on newspapers, magazines, radio or television. Those three were Burma Shave with signs, Goodyear with blimps, and Mail Pouch with barns."

Bloch is a descendant of the Blochs of Wheeling, who first started making cigars as a sideline product for their general store business in 1879 and began painting signs to extol their new product. The barn signs followed-- aimed again at the Bloch market, the rural and small town chewers.

The signs appearing today basically are unchanged from the ones of 70 years ago--the letters on a black background, the legend "Treat Yourself to the Best," all framed with a sky- blue border. Those painted words are so famous that one New York restaurant owner has paneled the interior of his establishment with wood from an old barn. The first thing one sees on entering is "Mail Pouch."

Bloch Bros. now has just one painter--Harley Warrwick-- instead of the crews that used to fan out over the countryside to paint barns all summer long.

Warrwick, whose home is Belmont, Ohio, has been painting for the company for 30 years. He is the only painter but he says he is not the last. Warrwick also is the advance man. That means he arranges everyting with the farmer to paint the barn (rent, paper work, licenses) before the crew, meaning Warrwick, arrives to paint it.

Listen to Warrwick:

"Well, uh, a farmer is naturally suspicious of anybody that comes in with a suit and shiny briefcase. He thinks, you know, it's someone working for a government agency or something, see.

"But if you go in there, you know, just an ordinary working man, and you just start talking to him about his crops, he's got a pretty good idea what you're there for--naturally with the 'Mail Pouch' on the side of the truck.

"But you start talking about his crops, about his hogs or his cattle or whatever he's raising. And finally you get around--like horse trading--you get around to talking about what you're there for.

"He knew it all the time what you was there for, but he don't want to mention it, you see. But we've had guys out from the company wearing suits, and they would come out and lease the space. They didn't last very long. They went out there with a big Oldsmobile and a briefcase and they started telling the farmer what they was going to do. You don't *tell* a farmer...."

As for sites, Warrwick says:

"Well, we try to stick more to industrial areas or, where there will be users of the product, in other words. The coal mines --naturally they can't smoke in the coal mines so they're going to chew. So, say, the guy chews some other brand of tobacco.

"He's chewed all his life as far as that goes. But he's riding down the road and he keeps seeing this Mail Pouch, Mail Pouch, Mail Pouch. And after a while, maybe he comes up short. He hasn't got a pack of tobacco. What's the first thing he's going to think of? It's going to be Mail Pouch, see?

"If he goes in a store, and then maybe he tries it, he'll keep on using it."

As for making calls, Warrwick recalls:

"It was down below Weston, W.Va. I don't know what the old fellow's name was, and he was an invalid and of course I didn't know that at the time. I went up and knocked on the door and he says, 'Come on in.'

"So I opened the door and pushed it back and here's a double-barreled shotgun pointed right at you, you know. He was old and shaky anyhow, you know. And he wanted to know, 'What you want?'

"And I told him.

" 'Oh, yeah,' he says. 'I remember you was here before.'

"I had painted there before. And finally--it seemed like it took him a year to get the shotgun back down where he could relax, you know.

"Then he says, 'Well, if it had been somebody trying to get me and my shotgun hadn't worked,' and he reached under the covers and started shaking around a big, old, long revolver.

"He had been robbed once before. Some guys came up there in broad daylight and robbed him. He couldn't get out of bed. So that's why he had the shotgun.

"He was tickled to death to get his barn painted. He wanted to know if I had any Mail Pouch. 'You got any samples out in the truck?' he says. So I went down and got him a carton. He said he chewed it all the time.

"He was a lonesome old guy, nobody there to take care of him. His son would come down and feed him twice a day and wash him up. And it got so every evening when I was done I'd stop and see if he needed anything and sat and talked to him for about an hour, you know."

There's one other thing about the traditional Mail Pouch barn sign. It has a sky-blue border, painted along corners and roofline of the barn on the end the sign's on.

It's Warrwick's finishing touch. As he explains:

"You have to have a border on it. It's like a picture without a frame, you know."

January 29, 1986

Army Was Road Out of Slavery

TIPTON, Mo. -- What's known about Fleming Stradford over the distance of 122 years is precious little. But there are a few things:

On July 22, 1864 -- when the Civil War's outcome still seemed chancy -- he came here to Tipton and "presented himself" to Union authorities. He was enlisted in the Missouri Colored Volunteers.

Young Stradford was 17, born in Pettis County, and was a farmer.

Naturally, since this was Missouri and he was black, Mr. Stradford was a slave. He was owned by E. C. Wooldridge of Boone County, who'd gotten him as part of an estate settlement.

A couple of other things. Mr. Stradford couldn't write. He marked his enlistment form with an "X."

And he was short, 5 feet 2 inches tall. You can almost picture the young man, a boy really, standing there before the soldiers, his chest pushed out with pride.

The enlistment meant more than marching and adventure to Fleming Stradford. It meant he was a free man. The "X" he scratched on the paper was his personal emancipation.

This coming month, school children all over the country will take part in black history studies. They will learn that black soldiers -- roughly 200,000 of them -- fought for the Union. Men like young Stradford.

And they will study how Abraham Lincoln freed the slaves with the Emancipation Proclamation.

What'll probably be passed over is that Mr. Lincoln didn't free all the slaves. His proclamation covered only slaves in areas under Confederate control. For slaves in Missouri and other border states where the Union had nominal power, slavery still was slavery.

Unless you enlisted. Or were drafted. The government was very careful about all that. Search the congressional records and you'll find no humanistic spirit--slavery was still a business. The U.S. government figured owners of slaves who enlisted were owed $300 in compensation; owners of drafted slaves were to get $100.

And after the war, Missouri slave owners, mostly residents of the river counties, applied for that compensation. They wanted their money.

The records of all this--applications, ownership records, affidavits, claim forms--are in about 30 folders at the Kansas City Branch of the National Archives.

How the folders were saved is almost as amazing as what's in them. Mark Corriston, a federal archivist, says the papers apparently were stored in the attic of the old Topeka federal building along with some material about Wild Bill Hickok and some German-Americans who were thought to be enemy agents in World War I.

The federal building was torn down in the early 1930s. And the records were bundled off to the Kansas State Historical Society. There they stayed until the Federal Archives acquired them.

As far as Mr. Corriston can determine, they are the only extant records anywhere of such compensation claims.

Not surprisingly, some of the names of the owners wanting payment for their slaves are still well-known in central Missouri -- people who endow colleges or head historical societies.

The names of the black men who fought for their country are more mundane--Mikey Anderson, John White, Joe Murphy, Nelson Turner, et al.

But they are more--they are the only record of forgotten men who somehow knew that donning the blue coat of their nation and marking their "X" promised them a better chance. Even if they had to die fighting.

"Most of the compensation forms are dated in 1867," Mr. Corriston says. "But there is no record of any claims ever being paid. I think what happened was that after the war the whole idea of paying people was dropped. Quietly and quickly. Even then it was a little too much."

October 28, 1982

Unsettling Picture of Settlers

LAWRENCE, Kan. -- Scott McNall has a picture in his mind's eye of a 19th century Great Plains settler, maybe a Kansan, maybe a Dakotan, standing beneath the huge, annihilating sky, knowing that his strong back was his only hedge against drought or blizzard, wind or hail.

There's nothing wrong with that image. It's true. Life's linchpin until 50 years ago was muscle power and 18-hour days.

Yet strangely, in the years since the plains were settled or the rolling dust clouds billowed across the land in the 1930s, a notion has evolved that all settlers and their descendants embodied the work ethic, raised large, well-behaved families, took care of their own, triumphed over natural adversity, were tolerant and worked together in a halo-light of bucolic good will.

'T ain't so, say Mr. McNall and his wife, Sally McNall, authors of the forthcoming book, *Sociology Through Social History: Great Plains Families, 1860-1980.*

The book, to be published in January by St. Martin's Press, uses diaries, letters, newspaper accounts and interviews with survivors of the so-called "good old days" to cast popular history of those days into varying shades of gray.

Among other things, the McNalls note:

· Tenacity wasn't the strong suit of many settlers. In the period between 1882 and 1887 over half the families in western Kansas simply packed up and left with some religious groups, taking a hard right somewhere near Wichita and ending up in Latin America.

· Family units had problems -- outright abandonment by fathers in the 1930s, settlers grudgingly taking in aged relatives (a separate dwelling was often built for them) and throwing the kids out of the house at a certain age.

· Big families, especially among rural Protestants, were the exception rather than the rule, with the average number of children in the 1890s hovering around three. There was a negative image of people who had several children, namely Catholics and foreign born.

• Tolerance often was given lip service. Catholics, unless within a Catholic community, suffered real persecution from their Plains neighbors. During World War I, German-speaking Americans were forced to end their use of the language by either state or municipal fiat or threat of violence.

• As for rural-town cooperation, documentation exists that the two groups often were bitterly opposed to each other with little or no compromise on either side. The issues were often picayune but very real -- townspeople floating a bond issue over protests of farmers to pave the town's streets, and the farmers ending up paying most of the tax bill.

That latter bitterness spilled into newspapers with the farmers viewing the townspeople as "an idle, unproductive" class and editors such as William Allen White of Emporia, Kan., branding the farmers as "the scum of the earth," opinions that run counter to the legend of good will.

Mr. McNall, the chairman of the sociology department at the University of Kansas, and his wife, a KU English instructor, don't discount the stories on the other side of the coin. Mr. McNall ran across one where a woman bought ice in town day after day, month after month, and took it home to the country, half melted by the time she got there, because ice packs gave a woman relative dying of cancer her only relief from pain.

Yet there was a darker side, rarely mentioned in history books -- suicide, divorce and mental illness.

"We have references in diaries of women having a nervous disposition, meaning they cried continually," Mr. McNall says. "I don't think we can imagine what some of these people went through on the Great Plains -- the isolation, the freezing wind, droughts, and then seeing your crops, everything you'd banked on, eaten by grasshoppers. It was spooky."

The thesis of the book is that people are the result of their historical environment, and the Great Plains -- because of the area's late settlement and religious, economical and political blend -- are unique. And not quite what the conventional history books say they are.

Oddly, in their research the McNalls never came across the phrase "the good old days."

"In our oral interviews people would talk about the past with a certain nostalgia, mainly about people," he says. "But if they mentioned going back, they made it understood that they wanted to go back with a lot of the modern conveniences they have today."

February 26, 1986

River Is Not What It Was

MALTA BEND, Mo. -- John T. Ewing remembers the way the river used to be. Miles wide at flood stage. Wide even in droughty times, parts shallow enough to almost wade across.

The Missouri River, The Big Muddy. Silt-laden. Ice-choked in winter. A place a boy could swim and fish and hunt. Or sit on the bank and stare, fascinated, at the coal-fired paddle-wheelers churning up river. Or churning nowhere when foundered on a sand bar.

Mr. Ewing can even recall the boats' names -- *Advance, Decatur, Chester.*

There were other boats. Snag boats searched the river for timber cut away from the banks by the river and tossed into the current. Those boats sought out the huge walnuts and other hardwoods that could be made into boards to build the houses and stores. Really, the towns.

But for Mr. Ewing one image of the river is stronger than all the others. That image is of ducks -- hundreds of thousands that literally darkened the sky. Back then -- this was about 1912 -- people didn't talk about flyways, routes ducks would take north or south every year. The ducks just came, fall and spring.

Now Mr. Ewing, who's 84, looks at the river and sees a ditch. A quarter mile wide or maybe a little more. Or a little less. It's the Missouri River, channeled into a thin ribbon of water by levees and revetments, jetties and riprap, all courtesy of the U.S. government.

Like the river, Mr. Ewing's world has changed. And only a few ducks come now.

"You just don't see them," he says. "The big, old river and all the little oxbow lakes and ponds left by it are gone. Where there were 100 mallards before, now you're lucky to see 25."

But being a thoughtful man, Mr. Ewing thinks the lessening of the duck population can be blamed only partly on the Missouri's diminution. Because when Mr. Ewing was a youth, farmers picked and shucked corn almost all fall and winter.

So there was food for the ducks. Farmers didn't care particularly for the hungry birds. But that was part of nature's rhythm. They put up with it. At least until corn headers on combines came along and fields could be swept clean in a day or two.

Of course, Mr. Ewing remembers, the ducks meant hunting.
His father was a "market hunter," one who supplied wild game to restaurant tables in Kansas City and St. Louis.

"We hunted all the time," says Mr. Ewing, who used to make duck decoys, objects that would have had collectors throwing money through his door now if he'd kept them all.

Naturally, Mr. Ewing couldn't survive making decoys. So he went to work on the river. Except for some farming, the river has been his life -- from the mouth of the Missouri north of St. Louis back west to Waverly, Mo. He and his wife, Ruth, lived in little river towns that are no longer on the map.

Three dollars a day. Cutting willows with an ax, then weaving them into revetments. Learning little things like diving deep if you fell off the boat laying the revetment, else the nails that held the branches would snag you. And drown you.

In a real sense, Mr. Ewing helped change the river he's always loved, making it deeper and navigable. "A ditch," as he now describes it.

Is it better or worse?

"Better," he says. "There's more game now -- turkey, deer, beaver."

And life is better. Not the constant struggle.

Still, there's hesitation in his voice. Mr. Ewing misses the ducks -- the sound of their calls, their wings beating against the wind as they came low over a majestic, untamed river that now has become no more than a tool of man.

January 12, 1992

Some Kansans Gave Custer's Cavalry Early Taste of Battle

CHETOPA, Kan. -- It's generally agreed that when Lt. Col. George Armstrong Custer and most of his 7th Cavalry bit the dust at the Little Bighorn in 1876, the United States went into a collective fit of shock, grief, anger and vengeance.

In the ensuing couple of decades, immigrant Americans did bad things to native Americans, herded what was left of the tribes onto reservations and acted in such a boorish manner that the Indians are still trying to get even.

They do that in a number of ways. One tiny effort now is selling bumper stickers saying rather raw things about Custer and the 7th up at Crow Agency, Mont., the nearest town to the Little Bighorn battlefield. That site, incidentally, is currently embroiled in a name change controversy. Indians want "Little Bighorn Battlefield National Monument" to replace "Custer Battlefield National Monument."

What all the above has to do with Chetopa in southeast Kansas may seem murky.

Except it was here, six years before the fight at the Little Bighorn, that Chetopa's citizens fought the U.S. 7th Cavalry to a standstill, then skinned them--not literally, but financially.

Naturally, what happened didn't ever make the history books. Nor did it end up on any bumper stickers.

It all started with one James F. Joy, a financier who makes the 1980s Wall Street sharks look like altar boys.

Joy was, in a word, rapacious. In 1867 be bought what was to be Crawford and Cherokee counties and started charging local squatters from $2 to $5 an acre for their land he didn't plan to use as right-of-way for the railroad he was building.

The settlers were not pleased. They started harassing survey crews, burning railroad equipment, threatening to hang work crews, and making themselves generally obnoxious. Kind of like the Indians who did in Custer.

Joy didn't fool around. He telegraphed Washington, and before you know it, four companies of the 6th Infantry and Company A of the 7th Cavalry were in southeast Kansas, dispatched by none other than President Ulysses S. Grant.

On Oct. 18, 1870, Company A established a camp on the outskirts of Chetopa to protect Joy's interests.

From official reports, newspaper files and government claim forms, historians Michael Guifoyle and Randy Kane have pieced together what happened next.

It was raining that day. The troopers, apparently weary of their tents, came into town and gathered at a saloon operated by Hiram Barnes.

Adult beverages were consumed--in quantity. The soldiers got knee-walking drunk.

When the barkeep tried to cut off the soldiers' libations, they, as drinkers are wont to do, protested. Blows were traded. A mirror was broken, followed by the plate-glass window. Finally the whole front of the joint was demolished.

Chetopa citizens, observing the razing of what to them was a beloved institution, seized several large-caliber weapons and blazed away. The troopers skedaddled back to camp, returned with carbines and shot up the town. Amazingly, no one was killed.

Eventually things settled down. The Army said the townspeople started the riot; the townspeople pointed their fingers at the Army and started adding up the damages.

The claims are interesting. The cracked mirror was charged at $80. A missing set of billiard balls was worth a whopping $25. One smashed billiard table was valued at $160. Liquor, spilled or stolen, was listed at $27, despite the fact that Barnes eschewed bonded bourbon or vintage wine.

The total came to $563, and the troopers had to pay it. Barnes, like future government claimants, tried for an additional $500, saying that soldiers had stolen 2,000 of his cigars. The government disallowed that, noting there probably weren't 2,000 cigars in this part of Kansas, let alone Chetopa.

As for the 7th and the Little Bighorn: Well, despite the rehearsal here, none of the enlisted men involved in the Chetopa fracas took part in the Montana tussle. Being enlisted and halfway smart, they got out of the Army as soon as they could.

One 7th Cavalry officer, with the improbable name of Algernon Smith, did die at the Little Bighorn. And the commanding officer of Company A that day here, one Sam Robbins? He was court-martialed and resigned from the Army in 1872. The reason? "Public drunkenness."

Figures.

May 21, 1983

Germans Mark Third Century

COLUMBIA, Mo. -- In case you missed it, there will be a tricentennial this year. Put July 4, 1776, away. This year's date is Oct. 6, 1683.

The tricentennial will mark the day 300 years ago that 13 German emigrants disembarked at Philadelphia from the packet *Concord*, wobbly-legged from the long ocean crossing. Those 13, most weavers of the Mennonite faith, were the first of a cascade of German immigrants to the United States.

Any talk of German immigration to this country must include Missouri. And, of course, it must include Adolf E. Schroeder, professor of German at the University of Missouri here, director of the Missouri Origins Project and a man up to his hips in a variety of statewide projects to honor the immigrants who at one time made up 40 percent of the state's population.

"Just about everybody," says Mr. Schroeder, an ebullient man with an infectious grin, "has a German grandmother."

The what and the why of those first German immigrants were fairly simple, contends Mr. Schroeder.

Lutherans and Catholics emerged paramount in what was a fragmented Germany late in the 17th century and found persecuting pious groups like the Mennonites great sport. When they weren't imprisoning or torturing them, the dominant faiths liked to sew minority sect believers into sacks and throw them in the nearest river. Thus 66-day boat trips and the chance of being lost in the Atlantic held little terror for emigrating Germans.

Still, things didn't start in Missouri until 140 years later. There had been sporadic settlement in the state -- German was the second language of Cape Girardeau in 1799. But it took the arrival of Gottfried Duden to get things off the ground.

With typical German practicality Mr. Duden bought a farm in Warren County in the mid-1820s and lived on it for three years. With Mr. Duden, an attorney, was Ludwig Evermann, whom Mr. Schroeder says can only be described today as an agricultural economist. Mr. Evermann oversaw the farm work, the planting of crops, putting in the orchards and construction of the fences, and he took care of the harvests. He found out what crops grew best, tallied profit and loss, then reported it all to Mr. Duden.

Mr. Duden apparently spent most of his time observing, reading and visiting folks. But underneath he was passionate about the overpopulation of Germany, which was still in ferment because of poverty, autocratic rule by the princes (although throwing people in rivers apparently had stopped) and heavy taxation.

Mr. Duden wanted Missouri to become a North American Germanic state. He wrote down what Mr. Evermann reported and in 1829 published a book called *Bericht uber eine Reise nach den Westlichen Staaten Nord Amerikas* (Report on a Journey to the Western States of North America).

In retrospect, says Mr. Schroeder, probably no single book ever written had the effect on Missouri, or the nation, that Mr. Duden's book had. It sold like hot cakes. Edition after edition was published in Germany and Switzerland. The book was passed from hand to hand, was devoured by anyone who could read and was responsible, scholars contend, for the massive surge in immigration to Missouri.

With the Germans came a work ethic that ranged from farming to the skilled trades; a fanatical zeal to organize towns and name places; a love of a culture that ultimately meant orchestras and a unique architecture; and, above all, an abhorrence of oppression.

Slavery was anathema to the immigrants. The Germans, who had become dominant in St. Louis, were the main reason Missouri stayed with the Union that fateful spring of 1861, a fact that, quite simply, shaped American history. Nine of the first 10 regiments responding to President Lincoln's call to arms were made up of Germans; their muster lists, still on file in Jefferson City, were written in German, not English.

In his book Mr. Duden wrote of the fertility of the land, advised immigrants to buy improved property to generate cash quickly with the crops, and told potential German newcomers to organize into groups, appoint leaders and send out scouts first to find their land. His readers did just that.

These letters to one such group, the Giessener society, have survived. Those folks had thought of settling in Arkansas.

"The society sent scouts but hadn't heard from them," says Mr. Schroeder, "so they made up their mind to leave anyway. Just before they were to get on the boat they heard from the scouts. The message was, 'Don't go to Arkansas, Arkansas is terrible.' So they settled in Missouri instead."

June 12, 1982

Culture Came Hard to Kansas

TOPEKA -- Buried in agate type in the newspapers last month was the fact that the Kansas Legislature appropriated $600,000 for public television--to bring culture to Kansas.

Fittingly, it was 100 years ago this spring that a 28- year-old Englishman trouped the boards of theaters in four Kansas towns telling Kansans in no uncertain terms about their lack of culture. From contemporary accounts, however, the best night that poet Oscar Wilde had in Leavenworth, Atchison, Lawrence, and Topeka--at least in terms of admissions collected--was about $30. The Kansans who trickled in to see Mr. Wilde and then sat on their hands were, as one writer put it, "Philistines -- unafraid and unapologetic, naive and bumptious, above all magnificently candid."

Culture, in short, came hard to Kansas, especially a century ago when the audiences sat there in their muddy boots and work clothes, spat tobacco and stamped their feet when they were bored. Bluntly, Kansas audiences demanded their money's worth.

A year earlier, in 1881, "the divine" Sara Bernhardt had played Kansas, leaving behind, as one wag put it, "her divinity all shot to hell and its tail feathers somewhat singed."

Miss Bernhardt, an actress who made European and Eastern American audiences curl in their toes in anticipation when she entered stage left, was described by Kansans as "distressingly ugly," a woman who had "arms like an octopus and walks like she had one joint in her body and no knees," and having a terrible figure. Ed Howe, the *Atchison Globe* editor, complained that she didn't even know how to kiss.

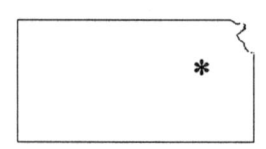

"She will soon sink out of sight," wrote Mr. Howe, "and then we will impatiently await the arrival of another foreign humbug."

Within a year Mr. Wilde had arrived from London by way of Colorado, where he'd had a delightful time touring the lead- mining regions of Colorado where he had outdrunk the miners in their saloons and even occasionally made them laugh in the opera houses with his discourses on the higher brackets of aesthetics, something he found woefully lacking in Americans.

Mr. Wilde, who arrived at Kansas City's Hickory street station, was, to say the least, a rather bizarre figure in a town in which the major municipal problem was the disposal of dead horses, cows, and hogs which seemed to litter every corner.

The Kansas City Times described Mr. Wilde as alighting from the train wearing pointed shoes, a velvet coat, lace cuffs, knee breeches, ribbons in his sleeves, a large jewel suspended from his neck, and dark hair washing over his shoulders. In one of this hands he carried a little yellow book of poems.

One newspaper described Mr. Wilde as "a pronounced and irreclaimable rainbow-hued ass." Another publication (in those days newspapers said what they thought) said Mr. Wilde's head was "pyramidal and tapers to a point."

The Times, however, reported that Mr. Wilde's talk that night had been "forceful." But the *Kansas City Journal* said it was "a tale told by an idiot full of sound and trash, signifying nothing."

In Kansas, Mr. Wilde found more of the same. Greeting him in Atchison was a dilapidated jackass parading up and down the main street with a placard on each side reading, "I lecture at Corinthian Hall tonight."

About 30 people showed up for the lecture on "decorative art," an aesthetic subject somewhat over the head of Atchison residents, since their big problem was the disposal of old dray horses who seemed destined to drop dead in the middle of town, not to mention raw sewage running in the streets.

"He finds our houses ugly, our surroundings dreadful," wrote crusty D.R. Anthony, the editor of the *Leavenworth Times*. "He is an uncommon cold."

The reception wasn't any better at the final two stops, Topeka and Lawrence. There, too, the sparse audiences listened and left. There is no record of any applause for Mr. Wilde in any of his Kansas appearances. As he left the state, one paper characterized him as "a distinguished clown."

Mr. Wilde never mentioned his Kansas experiences when talking of his American tour, the whole of which he recalled fondly. He probably didn't understand Kansans, nor did they understand him. The only record of any feeling he ever had toward his visit was when the residents of Griggsville, Kan., asked him to lecture to them on aesthetics.

"I replied," Mr. Wilde said later, "that you should begin by changing the name of your town."

August 27, 1983

Out of the Hands of Babes

HOLDEN, Mo. -- Over the years, this Johnson County, Mo., town of 2,100 has seemed, oh, contentious. At least to outsiders.

There'd be a City Council meeting and lots of shouting. Or a police officer would get fired and raise a ruckus. Then the Warrensburg or Kansas City paper would come down from time to time and write a piece about trouble in Holden.

The thing was that Holden was just noisy--a nice little town with ordinary problems that usually became public. And that seemed to make Holden different.

Well, maybe Holden is different. Holden's got Arthur Bachler.

Mr. Bachler, 61, is a big bear of a man, a McDonald County native from southwest Missouri, a World War II artilleryman and a retired civilian employee of the Missouri National Guard.

Mr. Bachler is Santa Claus, too. For the last 14 years he's been the Santa Claus at the Blue Ridge Mall in Kansas City, the man who comes in by helicopter every year, delighting the children, asking them if they've been good and ending his yearly visits by giving each child a big hug. A real hug, too.

"I just love kids," says Mr. Bachler, who has his own although they're grown and have moved away.

A year ago, being retired and at loose ends, Mr. Bachler figured he'd be Santa Claus 365 days a year to his adopted hometown of Holden.

If there's one thing about old Army warrant officers like Mr. Bachler, it's observation. He looked around in the summer of 1982 and saw that Holden's youngsters, ages 6 to 13, had almost nothing to do except just sit around on the front porch, maybe learn how to smoke cigarettes and maybe get into a little mischief. The kids were at that age, the time when their mothers would ask what they're doing and they'd say, "Oh, nothing."

Mr. Bachler thought about it and just a year ago announced his plan to form a new Holden youth organization. The idea was simple -- the kids would give of themselves and work on civic improvements, and in return they'd get all the free pop they could drink plus trips to go fishing and swimming and roller skating.

"Well, I told him he was crazy," says Eva Cast, civic chairman of the Holden Garden Club.

"No, I didn't think it would work," says Sherry Kane, a Holden paramedic who's worked with children.

Mr. Bachler says himself that "some thought it would work, a lot thought it wouldn't." Being somewhat like a bulldog that won't let go of what it's got between its teeth, Mr. Bachler forged ahead. He walked miles around town, asked merchants for donations to get things going, put out boxes in food stores so people could donate canned foods and other necessities to needy families.

The boxes were Mr. Bachler's ace in the hole. As an observer of human nature he figured he had to bridge the gap of teaching the kids how to give rather than take. One of the first acts of the youth club, now called the Eagle Recruit Organization, was to pass out food and toys to 13 needy families at Christmas last year.

"I knew once those kids looked in the eyes of people they were giving things to, I'd have them," says Mr. Bachler. "Some of these kids had never given away anything in their lives."

The organization, which Mr. Bachler asserts "is Holden's, not mine," has grown like Topsy, with more than 100 children from first to seventh grade now in its ranks.

The Eagle Recruits keep the outside of the community building clean. They help serve meals to senior citizens. They weed the several small parks around town, much to the delight of Mrs. Cast. They help wash the fire trucks. They've grown a garden and given the produce away. So far they've scoured every street in Holden for trash and debris, some several times.

And every Sunday morning, with Mr. Bachler in the lead, the kids are picking up the Saturday night trash from First Street. Listen to Mayor Don Hancock:

"I was down one Sunday morning, and one of those little kids said to me, 'Hey, mayor, this town may be a little dirty, but we're getting it cleaned up, aren't we?' "

Mr. Bachler says the Eagle Recruit program could be repeated in every town in Missouri and every neighborhood of the state's bigger cities.

"Kids want something to do," he says. "Sure they like to swim and fish and play. But watch a kid play and then project ahead a few years and you're really watching an adult work.

"The thing is, though, you've got to get 'em young."

July 26, 1991

History, in This Book, Is What People Talk About

GARNETT, Kan. -- County histories used to be a big deal--thick, hardbound books; maybe some pictures of the wealthier citizens; what churches and schools were where; articles about fraternal lodges; who the local sawbones were; and the names of various confidence men posing as lawyers.

Dry stuff. But in the late 19th and early 20th centuries, such histories sold like hotcakes.

In recent years several Missouri and Kansas counties have come out with new books, most of them equally dry unless your or a relative's name is in it. They're also sanitized. Dull.

So it's rare that you see history like this:

Charley Farrow, rushing home from hunting, stood his shotgun in the corner. His pet circus monkey saw him. . . and when Charley left grabbed the loaded gun and ran out the door.

He climbed on the woodpile by the clothes line. The monkey, playing with the automatic shotgun, accidently touched the trigger. And BOOM, it blew a hole in Mrs. Farrow's Sunday go-to-meeting bloomers.

Mrs. Farrow, seeing what happened, grabbed a broom and walloped the monkey over the head.

History? Well, maybe not to some ivory tower academic. But you can bet people talked about the shotgun-toting simian long after they remembered who was elected county prosecutor in 1912.

The monkey story is the kind of history Ed Fink specializes in. His 201-page *Pictorial History and Folklore of Anderson County, Kansas, From Earliest Times to World War II* is full of such stories.

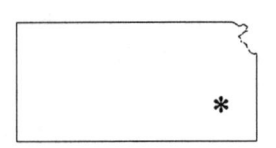

And that's right--the book is "pictorial." The monkey story is accompanied by five drawing showing exactly what Fink thinks happened, including the hole in the bloomers. Ed not only researches, collates and analyzes, he draws and letters.

"The people who've been buying it are younger folks," said Ed. "Older ones haven't gotten around to stopping by. But they will."

Ed, 79 and retired, was a barber here for years and years. And a guy who's loved history. He's also a pretty fair cartoonist who once worked for Dr. John Brinkley, the goat gland doctor. Another thing--he's a musician who makes his own instruments.

Anyway, every now and then Ed would write a little story about some event, illustrate and letter it, then hang it on the wall of his shop.

For years, Dr. Robert Stevens, a local physician, was after Ed to publish a book. Finally Stevens became the publisher and Ed did the book in the kitchen of his home at 316 E. Third St. The first printing was 500. In three weeks nearly 200 have been sold at $21 each.

"I was lucky to have come along when some of the old-timers were still alive and remembered way back," said Ed. "So a lot of the book is firsthand.

"Then there was this guy named Harry Johnson who wrote a county history in the '30s. I helped him. We'd sit there and he'd look at a story and throw it in the wastebasket. 'Too controversial,' he'd say. And I'd get into the trash and keep all the stuff he threw away. And that's in the book.''

A lot of what was considered controversial is how over the years Anderson County was a haven for outlaws, namely William Quantrill, Jesse James and Pretty Boy Floyd. In fact, Ed said, the old Jesse James house (oddly enough the first prefabricated residence ever erected in the county) still stands south of here near Bush City.

"People didn't used to want to hear things like that," Ed said.

Judging from the sales of the book, they apparently do now. People like the hundreds of cartoons. And the stories. The copy, if sometimes a tad trite, is nonetheless history that people talk about.

Like Zack Taylor, lighting his pipe and throwing a match down the unoccupied part of a two-holer, being literally blown through the door of the outhouse.

Or how in 1938 Ben Cote's Duroc sow farrowed a pig with seven feet. Soon afterward a sow of similar breeding belonging to Jim Edwards gave birth to one with eight feet.

Or how the first highway through here was between Tulsa and Kansas City and was marked not with a number but with a picture of an oil derrick tacked to telephone poles.

That kind of stuff.

You know, history.

August 22, 1981

Doomsayer Foresees a Famine

HOLT, Mo. -- As G.W. Admires sees it, there are maybe 10 or 15 years left. After that, unless things change, get ready for famine and pestilence.

"Nuclear war will look like child's play," says Admires, a man who predicts the weather but who with his stentorian voice and dire warnings hardly sounds like a television forecaster. "By 1990, you'll see the first" of the famine.

Admires is a big, white-haired man of 58, including 27 years in the U.S. Navy, regular and reserves, and he draws a disability pension. He says government-financed weather modification is leading to disaster not just in the United States but all over the world. Among other things, he claims, such modification has caused:

· Last year's drought and this year's rain.

· Three years of bad harvests in the Soviet Union.

· Almost surely the 1977 Brush Creek flood in Kansas City, probably the 1951 flood on the Kansas River and decidedly the Big Thompson Canyon flood in Colorado a decade ago.

And maybe, Admires says, just maybe, weather modification caused the horrendous 1903 Missouri River flood.

"You know, Congress passed the first weather modification law in 1902," he hints darkly, adding that such modification has been increasing steadily for the past 30 years but only a few people make the connection between recent weather anomalies and man-made weather.

Admires, who between stints as a Navy quartermaster specializing in meteorology was a bus driver in Kansas City and California, admits he lacks weather instruments at his home east of Holt. His forecasts, sent weekly to two Missouri newspapers and a Raytown ecological farming magazine, are based on his readings, he says.

"Public Law 92-205 requires people modifying weather to make reports," Admires says. "By reading those reports and putting it together with what I know or have read, I make forecasts."

Since the weather modifiers are seeding atmosphere out in western

Kansas, eastern Colorado and west Texas--"cloud busting" as Admires calls it--dry weather is his short range forecast for this area.

And the long-range forecast?

"A cold winter," Admires says. "Buy wood."

Admires, who says he's been called a "nut" for his theories, has a simple thesis. "They," a group he defines as government, big business and large acreage ranchers and farmers, are constantly seeding the atmosphere with silver iodide, dry ice, urea, acetone and metallic substances to cause rain or suppress hail.

Admires says 1979 figures of the National Oceanic and Atmospheric Administration show a total of 1,200 instances of seeding the atmosphere that year by various governmental and private agencies.

Then Admires points to a study published by the National Science Foundation that says, in part, there is "a new program in the Agricultural Weather Modification program...for exerting influence on agricultural systems at critical points during planting, growing, and harvesting."

"That," Admires says, "is a very significant statement." The 1908 drought, he adds, was caused by the weather modifiers' desire for a big wheat harvest. This year's rain is being used to fill reservoirs depleted by last year's drought and ensure a big corn crop for export, something commodity traders want because of the predicted Soviet grain crop shortfall in 1981, Admires says.

Admires contends that he isn't totally against weather modification. But, he says, the earth must be viewed as an organic whole. Because more than 60 nations (including the U.S.S.R.) have weather modification programs, the whole thing has degenerated into a willy-nilly race to see who can get what rain out of what clouds. Weather modification, he adds, must be done with finesse and in small amounts, not just by dumping tons of material into the atmosphere.

The simple truth, Admires says, is that the nations of the world are warring with one another because of weather modification.

"I'm for a moratorium on weather modification," he says. "Let the world get all that stuff out of the atmosphere. I'm for reporting what the effects of weather modification are going to be before they're done, not after. If you have to file an environmental impact statement to build a road, why not to change the weather?

"And I want young people to read up on the subject. They'll see I'm right. And they're the ones that will be affected in the future."

August 17, 1987

Old House Will Get a New Look

PITTSBURG, Kan. -- As houses go, the two-story, gabled structure here at 410 W. Kansas is doing, in a word, poorly. The green roof is molting, and the brick-red exterior paint appears to have eczema.

Weeds and brush have engulfed the house in the roughly two years it has been unoccupied, a state caused by certain financial difficulties. Cats found their way in, leaving their calling cards and a host of fleas.

That's not all. The roof leaks, the west wall of the structure is so saturated from moisture that it bulges, and mushrooms and lichens grow unbidden on the first floor.

Frankly the house has a long way to go before it's featured in either *Better Homes and Gardens* or *Architectural Digest*.

So why was Connie Corbett-Whittier absolutely beaming when she walked into the home of Pat Martin the other day and announced, yes, the bank had agreed to lend enough money to buy the house which, incidentally, is directly across the alley from the Martins', and not really that far from the Corbett-Whittier residence?

What's going on here? Are these two women sort of a neighborhood urban renewal authority? Is there something people ought to know about the house? And how do President Reagan and the perennially congested Ozarks resort town of Branson, Mo., fit into all this?

Simple. The house at 410 W. Kansas is the old Harold Bell Wright home. It needs saving, and Corbett-Whittier, Martin and others in the Little Balkans Heritage Preservation Guild are putting their money where their hearts are, buying the dilapidated home for $4,500, planning its renovation and hoping that within a few years, it'll be a Pittsburg showplace.

Harold Bell Wright? Who was he?

Wright, for the uninitiated, was the man who almost single-handedly created the Ozarks, as they are known today. He wrote, among other things, *The Shepherd of the Hills*, which established the image for Ozark behavior and dress-- slouch hat, flannel shirt, close-mouthed, reliant. No matter if John Wayne really didn't seem comfortable in allegedly homespun garments in the 1951 movie. Wayne's attitude was what counted. Ozarks is Ozarks.

Wright, who by 1910 had become the first million-dollar author in world history, wrote *The Shepherd of the Hills* at Branson. But his first book, *That Printer of Udell's*, sort of a Horatio Alger work that President Reagan has said exerted a profound influence on his life, was written in the sunlit study of the house here at 410 W. Kansas.

That book launched Wright's literary career. Up to then he'd been just a popular preacher here. It was the first of a cascade of books (and 17 subsequent film treatments) that made Wright's name a household word in the first half of this century.

"The house is historically significant," said Gene DeGruson, a guild member. "That's the reason we want to save it. Wright always said his five years in Pittsburg were the happiest time of his life. He married here. Most of his children were born here."

It's going to take work, Corbett-Whittier and Martin said. And money above and beyond the purchase price of the home-- probably an additional $5,000 to $18,000.

"But you'd be surprised how much volunteer labor can accomplish," Martin said. "Why, just the other night we cut a path to the house. Sure, it was like a jungle. But it was a first step."

November 5, 1981

Old-time Religion Airs Well

SARCOXIE, Mo. -- Their Ozark twang is on the radio from Muleshoe, Texas to South Africa. The strains of the old gospel music they play beams out across Panama, West Germany, and parts of the Soviet Union. And they're heard even in such diverse locales as Sri Lanka, Springfield, Mo., and Los Angeles.

"Not bad for a couple of Missouri hayseeds," says the Rev. Paul E. Smith, referring to himself and his wife, Mulva, both in their early 70s, who 11 years ago decided to retire and produce a religious broadcast for a couple of Sarcoxie area stations.

Now they're busier than ever, heard throughout a good part of the world on their "Old Country Church Radio Broadcast."

"It's just a few," says Mr. Smith, a spare, balding Holiness minister who also happens to be a chicken farmer. He figures that he's preached 9,000 times in the last 50 years, far short of the 40,000 sermons given by the founder of Methodism, John Wesley, whom Mr. Smith admires greatly and often mentions in his broadcasts. Mr. Smith isn't a Methodist, though; he's affiliated with an Independence, Kansas, Holiness group.

"We don't speak in tongues or do any of that stuff," Mr. Smith says. "We preach the Lord's Word and try to help our fellow man."

And when the time for an accounting comes, Mr. Smith says, he wants to be known for a couple of things: being a good evangelistic Christian, and being a radio preacher who "was on the level."

"Now you won't catch me saying anything against any radio preachers 'cept maybe ones who knock all the other preachers and figure they've got the only answer," Mr. Smith says.

"But a few radio preachers don't pay their bills. You go ask these radio stations who they have the toughest time collecting from, and they'll tell you preachers. A lot of stations want their money up front. That's a fact."

Mr. Smith, like other radio preachers, buys time on radio stations all over the country for broadcasts of the tape-recorded programs that he produces himself. He's got his program rules: have lots of features that appeal to a wide audience, and stay out of politics. Politics are poison for a radio preacher, he says.

He puts no price tag on the 30 minute broadcasts that he sends to radio stations overseas.

That's "missionary work," he says, and it gets results. Hundreds of letters from all over the world thanking the couple for the broadcasts are displayed in the Smith home.

"Most of those folks write better than I do," Mr. Smith says, laughing. "One thing is, though, even though I spell it out over the air, they can't seem to get 'Sarcoxie' or 'Missouri' right."

Variations of Sarcoxie's spelling have included Sorcoxtie, Sarcocci, Fartosie, Soar Coxcie, DstVocir and St. Cocksim. Missouri has been spelled Morsoua, Bezura, Mijor, McZorrie and Moosoorie.

In addition to the spellings sometimes being off the mark, several of the letters have been addressed to "The Old County Church Bells," or variations thereon, a tribute to the popularity of the bells of Granby, Mo. church that Mr. Smith tape recorded as he rang them. The sound of the bells kicks off his fast-paced program.

"You could say we're corny," Mr. Smith says. "Or country. But I don't mind that. We're just an old-time country church. We have a little singing; my wife tells a children's story; there's a brief sermon. Mulva plays the piano or organ and I play the tenor banjo, and we read the mail. Sometimes we just talk about the weather.

"Stations say we're the most popular religious program they have 'cause we're just common folks. It shows. Visitors--really listeners--roll in here at all hours just to say hello and say they hear us in New Jersey or California or Georgia."

Noticeably absent from the Smiths' program are the constant financial exhortations of some radio preachers.

Mr. Smith says $70,000 of his own money has gone into the broadcasts since 1970. On the program he'll ask maybe once or twice for contributions. But he tells listeners if they can't donate, write anyway and he'll send them a monthly bulletin and cassette recordings of past programs.

"The chickens help," he says, nodding at the brooder houses that contain 40,000 Leghorn layers. "We don't take a salary. Whatever our listeners send in goes to buy more radio time or do the missionary work. And that's the way it should be.

"You shouldn't get rich working for the Lord."

Memories Make Land Live Again

GYPSUM, Kan.-- At first glance the land hereabouts appears empty--not desolate but just empty, what with people leaving the farms over the years as machinery got bigger and managers more efficient. Towns like Gypsum, Assaria, Kipp, and Bridgeport have contracted a little each year as people went off to Salina to do their shopping.

Even the youngsters here usually think of the land as empty. And that was the way 10 juniors and seniors at Southeast of Saline High School thought about it last fall as they sat in on the first meeting of Mike Burcin's oral history class.

Oh, they said to themselves, this is is going to be a snap. No books. No lectures. None of that dry stuff about Dred Scott and Reconstruction and Marbury vs. Madison.

It didn't turn out that way.

"I don't think any of us have ever worked so hard at anything," Ingrid Blomquist said.

"We told them that this wasn't the kind of course that you could cram for the last week," said Charlotte Skinner, the school librarian who worked with Mr. Burcin on the course. "They had to get to work, and they did."

The assignments appeared easier than they were. All the kids had to do was interview people, look at original records, and find photographs. Brian Moses would write the history of the town of Kipp; Ingrid would write about Bridgeport; her cousin, Brian Blomquist, would write about Assaria; and Laura Fritz would write about Gypsum.

Gary Olson and Dwight Conley would write about the change from horses to tractors in the area; David Tilberg and Steve Mayer would write about the World War II Italian and German prisoner-of-war camp near Smolan; and Kurt Shaw and Lantz Forsythe would write about a similar camp for German officers just north of Concordia.

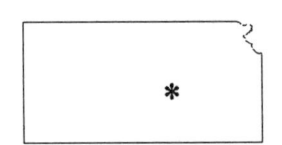

"Well, it was something to see," Mr. Burcin said. "They started a little slow and had a hard time getting people to talk. But they stuck with it."

Ingrid added: "You'd call people up and tell them what you were doing, and they had a hard time understanding that you were interested in them. They didn't think a kid could be interested in anybody as old as they are. And at first they said that the stuff they knew wasn't important, you know, small-town stuff. But once you got them going, they talked a blue streak.''

Maybe that was the hardest part, Laura said--making contact. But the students showed an ingenuity in finding those contacts that Mr. Burcin still doesn't quite understand.

''You know, you sort of figured they'd talk to neighbors and relatives and things like that,'' he said. ''Not these kids. They'd go to supermarkets and Laundromats and leave notes on the bulletin boards asking anybody who knew something about their subject to call them. Can you believe historians leaving messages in Laundromats?''

That wasn't all. This being a media age, the kids talked or bluffed their way into local television and radio stations or went down to the local paper asking to be interviewed.

All fall, between the news and football scores, there were these little announcements asking people who knew anything about the old prisoner-of-war camp or anything that had ever happened at Kipp or Assaria to call such-and-such.

At one point, the Tilberg-Mayer team came up with a contact in Germany and were all ready to make a long-distance call there. But they never could get through on long distance.

Laura said people were flattered to find out a teen-ager cared. ''And if you were going to do a good job, you had to care,'' she said. Her research led her to the fact that in 70 years Gypsum has achieved a dubious record in Kansas: it has suffered more than 70 floods.

Little things happened. Ingrid asked a man in Bridgeport to draw her a rough map of the town, just to give her an idea of how the town was when there were more than 100 people in it plus stores, a lumberyard and other long-departed businesses.

When Ingrid went back the man had drawn her a map, a massive, detailed creation out of cardboard, pinpointing everything in town, done all from memory. She, like all the other students, found the land hadn't always been empty.

The result of a semester's work was presented earlier this month: well-researched tape and color slide productions complete with narration, the actual words of those interviewed and background music.

Not surprisingly, everybody in the class got an A.

September 2, 1990

Persistent Mob Accomplished Alcoholic Lynching

OSAGE CITY, Kan. -- It's a given in the history of the Old West that lynching usually was carried out with a length of hemp rope, a nearby tree, and a convenient horse. Or maybe, in a pinch, a horse-drawn buckboard.

Leastways that's what Hollywood has foisted on the public all these years. What western worth its salt didn't have somebody tying a hangman's knot, and then leering at the intended victim?

Reality was a little different. As often as not the varmint was just taken out and shot. Or thrown off a bridge with a greasy lariat around his neck. Face it--nice, 2- inch-thick ropes weren't something everybody carried around in his saddle bags.

So there was variety. And no more so than here when, just more than 100 years ago, a man was lynched with a glass of beer.

Well, not just one glass. A glass and a bottle of beer. The results of which were as fatal as any rope or shotgun.

What happened was this:

Early in the morning of June 23, 1890, S.B. Pettee and his wife were fast asleep in their home at Sixth and California streets here. Mrs. Pettee apparently had an early warning system akin to an AWACS plane. She awoke, punched her husband and announced:

"There's a man in the house. Shoot!"

Mr. Pettee, like any well-trained husband, produced the five-shot revolver he always slept with and began to blaze away at two indistinct figures lurking in the bedroom. They fired back, bullets from their weapons puncturing the bed, blowing up lamps, shattering pictures hung on the wall. Despite all the firepower, the Pettees emerged unscathed.

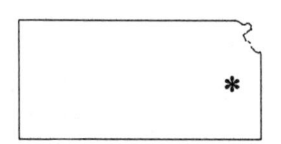

Pettee was a better shot than the burglars. They crashed out of the house. One disappeared into the night, but the other, wounded in the stomach, was found a block and a half away moaning, "I'm done for."

The burglar was identified as one Jim Curtis, 32, a resident of Michigan who apparently had been making nocturnal visits to various houses here and elsewhere in Kansas. He was transported to the City Hall because Osage City, at that point in its history, did not have a trauma unit or life-flight heliport to Topeka. At City Hall, Dr. W.L. Schenck examined him.

Indeed, Dr. Schenck discovered, Jim did have a considerable hole in his belly. Writing later in the *Kansas Medical Journal* Schenck reported he and other physicians gave the patient a large drink of whiskey, then "etherized" him. In a 45-minute operation, they opened him up, repaired four holes in various parts of his innards, swabbed him out with a solution of iodine, then sewed him up. The bullet, which couldn't be located, was left in him.

All this was done in the City Hall with a huge, muttering crowd looking on. Several people made the comment that the operation was a waste of time. What needed to be done was to hang the man, they said. One gets the impression reading Dr. Schenck's account that the operation was performed in a rather bizarre atmosphere.

Say this for the skill of Dr. Schenck and his colleagues--Jim started to recover. His biggest complaint was that he was given nothing to eat or drink. But that was the prescribed treatment.

For four days Jim made progress. Then one of the spectators, whether out of sympathy or possibly by design, slipped Jim a glass of beer. Which Jim, apparently a man familiar with strong beverages, drank.

The result was to be expected. Jim started vomiting. Dr. Schenck feared that the stitches inside had been torn loose. But no, once that episode was over, Jim came around and started his steady improvement again.

Well, if a glass did that, how about a little more? Two days later one of the townspeople gave Jim a bottle of beer, which he sucked down before the doctors could stop him.

That did it. Jim became violently ill. He was racked with convulsions. Dr. Schenck said he was sure all the stitches had been torn away. He was right, and Jim died July 5. The cause was peritonitis.

The autopsy showed that the bullet was safely tucked away in part of Jim's gut where it probably would have stayed for years and never given him a moment's trouble.

Dr. Schenck said he was sure the patient would have recovered except for "a City Hall open to the public for a hospital and a city government that desired the death of the patient."

See? Folks here didn't need a rope after all.

May 29, 1978

Scholar's Origins in Missouri

PIERCE CITY, Mo. -- The young man had the dust and manners of southwest Missouri on him when he left here 60 years ago.

When he died--just over a year ago in Bellingham, Wash.--the youth was an elderly man of 75, the dust of Missouri replaced by polished European manners from years of living abroad.

His name was William Newman. At the time of his death he was considered one of the greatest world authorities on French medieval history.

What brought about the change from the callow youth to the expert on 14th century France and the machinations of kings and princes will probably never be known. Newman was, in the words of an acquaintance, "a very private man."

The transformation was not without precedent, at least for this part of Missouri. Scant years before Newman left Pierce City, another young man left Nashville, Mo., 40-odd miles to the northwest.

His name was Harlow Shapley and he became the dean of American astronomers. Among other things he measured the known universe and found it to be 1,000 times larger than previously thought.

Apparently Newman's ability to adapt was there all along. After he left here to attend Phillips Academy in Andover, Mass., he bloomed, especially under the tutelage of Guy Forbush, the bespectacled terror of the French department. Forbush believed French should be taught in French, never English; use of the Anglo-Saxon tongue in a Forbush class was simply not tolerated.

Newman's record at Andover is spare; his graduation picture shows a serious, dark-haired youth looking directly at the camera, unsmiling.

Andover was followed by Harvard; Newman took undergraduate and graduate degrees there.

He was not poor. He could study where and when he wanted. Nor was his family poor. His grandfather, Joseph Newman, had founded a mercantile store in Pierce City in 1869 when the town was at the end of the railroad tracks. The Newmans were German immigrants then, hard working and acquisitive. Other stores followed--one in Enid, Okla., another in Joplin. Many say the latter is *the* department store in Joplin even today.

From Harvard, Newman went abroad, receiving doctorate degrees from the University of Toulouse and the University of Strasbourg.

In between he taught briefly at Ohio State. But he always returned to France, living while studying in Toulouse at an ill-heated hotel just around the corner from Antoine Saint-Exupery, the aviator and writer.

Toulouse and Strasbourg were followed by work at the University of Orleans in the early 1930s. In 1937 Newman published his first major work, *Le Domaine Royale sous les Premiers Capetiens*. It was critically acclaimed in France.

The book was dedicated to Guy Forbush--the man who had awakened the intellectual curiosity of the youth from Pierce City.

Eventually he published, in French, *Les Seigneurs de Nesle en Picardie*" a work that further enhanced his scholarly reputation.

Newman's works in medieval French history "are the absolute standards in the field," says Harvard Professor Giles Constable.

Newman is the only American to have his works in the Bibliotheque Nationale in Paris. Constable will oversee the publication of Newman's remaining, unpublished works.

Newman never married. A relative remembered that he was intensely devoted to his studies.

"One time the family sent him a watch and he sent it right back," the relative said. "He said he didn't need it. His time was taken up with studying medieval history and sleeping. What would he need a watch for?"

A nephew, Richard Newman, remembered his uncle as a gentle, solitary and serious man, "not the sort of uncle you would throw a baseball with." In his last letter to his nephew, Newman wrote wistfully of being back in Europe but said he had had his day "and must be satisfied."

Newman died in April 1977 at his home in Bellingham. Apparently he didn't forget those long-ago days when as a young man he stepped from the Boston and Maine Railroad car at Andover and found, perhaps in Guy Forbush's French classes, his destiny in life.

Newman left the whole of his estate--$750,000--to Phillips Academy. He put no restrictions on its use.

November 25, 1987

A Memory Lane, This Road Is

YATES CENTER, Kan. -- What's at Bell and North Main streets here looks not unlike a tombstone -- an angled granite marker facing southeast. A bronze plaque attached to the face of it has this legend:

       Memorial Road
  Women's Federation of Clubs
           1928

Actually, the marker isn't something you'd notice. It just sits there on the northwest corner of the street.

And what does it mean?

Well, on the surface, it doesn't mean a road unless you stretch your imagination.

It means, quite simply, an ordinary sidewalk. Once a mile long, heading north along North Main from Bell, past Skinner and Depew and Oak.

It heads into what used to be country pastures, land now transformed into lots where modern homes sit.

It means old-looking concrete, more brown than gray, but mixed well enough to have lasted almost 60 years.

It means a walkway to the Yates Center cemetery, a place a mile northwest of town surrounded by massive cedar trees.

But the "Memorial Road" really means more than that. It represents another way of life, a slower time when people didn't depend on cars for everything, and where cemeteries and the passing of a loved one were part of life's fabric.

Actually, the "Memorial Road" is a dinosaur, a part of Yates Center hardly known to most residents until a short newspaper article not long ago mentioned the pathway.

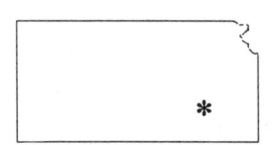

Gussia Schindler, who lived 20 miles north at Gridley, Kan., saw the little story and the memories flooded back to her -- of how in her youth the cemetery was the pride and joy of Yates Center, how school children used to walk out there on Sunday afternoons, their lips moving as they recited the names on the markers, of picnics and family gatherings at the burial ground.

Cemeteries then weren't spooky. places. They were where the living remembered and a bond tethered the young with those who'd gone before.

So Gussia -- her name used to be a fairly common Christian name -- got busy, driving here and scanning the microfilm of the Yates Center papers, talking to old-timers, remembering.

What Gussia, who's only 85, found out was that few had cars in the 1920s. That back then people walked most everywhere. And the most natural thing in the world to do on Sundays was to visit those who'd passed on.

The impetus for the sidewalk came when people, especially the older ones, found that the road out to the cemetery made for hard walking. And that the few newfangled motor cars here, speeding by the walkers, billowed dust or sprayed mud.

So the Yates Center womenfolk got together, especially after the men on the town council had pooh-poohed the whole idea.

In about a year, the ladies and their clubs raised the money. It was done in a variety of ways: clubs competing against clubs; tin cans placed in stores for contributions by those who didn't have a club membership; and what was called a "penny an inch" promotion, meaning one cent would pay for one inch of paving.

Eventually, $1,854.25 was in the pot. And the sidewalk was built.

The sidewalk was finished on Memorial Day 1928. It was dedicated on Armistice Day that same year.

"Most people have no idea about that sidewalk," Gussia said. "Build it today? Don't be silly. There'd be all sorts of paper work and federal block grants or something.

"In fact, that's what you've got to like about those old- timers. They saw something that needed doing and they just did it."

May 24, 1975

Mules Still Kicking in Old-timer's Memories

LATHROP, MO. -- A few years back, when the speaker for the Lathrop Rotary club didn't show up, C.L. Van Buren, a farmer who lives just west of here, got up and spoke. His general subject was Lathrop, but specifically he talk about horses and mules.

Van Buren talked about sugar mules, cotton mules, and pack mules; about artillery and cavalry horses, and how from 1914 to 1918 the land hereabouts was black with horses and mules, and how the dried manure from the pastures easily ignited and smoldered for days, leaving a pall of smoke over the area.

When Van Buren was finished the old-timers in the room merely nodded: they'd remembered. But others in the room, mostly city-bred folks who commute to Kansas City, were slack-jawed--awed by the numbers, the quantities of hay and feed, and most of all by the picture Van Buren painted of what Lathrop, now a prosaic Clinton County town, had been--a town surrounded by neighing and braying animals, where clipped British accents were common and $1-million bank drafts were carried around with ease.

Van Buren was pleased by the reception his off-the-cuff talk had received. But he also was disquieted.

"It seemed," Van Buren said yesterday, "like some of the newcomers had never even considered that the land had been used before. It's as if they thought it had always been gently rolling land covered with wheat or corn or beans. I felt like part of all we had worked for and done was slipping away--people had either forgotten or didn't know."

Although disquieted, Van Buren didn't let the newcomers' surprise bother him. He is 83, quick and alert, planning ahead, but more than willing to talk about the past--not a tintype past, but an active past--one with real people, real events.

"I came here in 1912," he said, "and needed work like everybody else. Here in Lathrop was the main station of Guyton & Harrington, the biggest mule and horse buyers in the world. Mostly they dealt in mules, picking up young 3-year-olds that just about every farmer raised as replacements. They'd get those mules in the fall of their second year, fresh with harness marks meaning they were broke to a team, fatten and get them slick up here, and sell them off down in Kansas City.

"I signed on with Mr. J.D. Guyton. He was a fine man and a good businessman. Guyton & Harrington had sold a lot of mules and horses to the British during the Boer War but when I came it was a domestic market. Sugar mules were big mules--we'd sell those down to the sugar cane plantations down South. Cotton mules were kind of medium and they went to the cotton fields. And pack mules were even smaller, about 14 hands (56 inches at the withers) and they went to the mountains or mines.

"By the time 1914 came along I was general foreman of the station here at Lathrop. And, of course, the British came, wanting all the mules and horses we could provide them. Guyton & Harrington had buyers out scouring the whole countryside, buying up everything that was sound.

"Well, you ask why did they need all those horses and mules and I'll tell you. Artillery fire. That killed a lot of them. And life at the front, once everybody got dug in, was especially hard on stock. It's easy to forget today that they didn't have big trucks and Jeeps and bulldozers in those days. They had mules and horses and they did about everything.

"Anyway the British came and the market was good and Guyton & Harrington pretty soon had 4,700 acres up around here, just about surrounding Lathrop. You know where the school is? That was Station No. 2. And right across the road from me, well, that was No. 18.

"Talk about a busy place. You drove in on M-116, a nice, quiet Missouri highway. Well, I can remember when it wasn't paved and it was choked with either horses or mules, driving people in carriages into the fields.

"Or take feed. We had silos full of feed all over the place and we'd load them with carload after carload of oats, corn and bran. And four days later they would be empty and I'd be looking down the track waiting for the next freight. There were days, especially when feed came in--plus carloads of horses and mules from out West of up North--that we'd move more cars and the Kansas City Terminal Railway.

"How many horses and mules? Well, we really never counted but I suppose that on any given day between 1914 and 1918 there were 30,000 in the fields around Lathrop.

"I don't remember what the average price was but something sticks in my mind like $150 but that may not be right. Anyway, Guyton & Harrington sold a lot and I remember this one little fellow named Arbuckle who dressed kind of seedy but was good with figures. He took the train down to Kansas City one day to deposit some money in the Commerce Bank and he came back saying that everybody there kind of turned up their noses at him because of the way he was dressed.

"Arbuckle, and I can't recall his first name, kind of tip-toed around for awhile until they got to him and then he pulled out a British check for over a million dollars payable to Guyton & Harrington and said he'd like to deposit it and all those Kansas City bankers fell all over themselves calling him 'Mr. Arbuckle.'

"There were a lot of British officers in Lathrop and I imagine they thought the Missouri way of doing things was kind of different than the way they did things in England. But everybody got along. Everybody. The riders that drove the horses were both black and white men and there wasn't any trouble. Everybody just worked.

"Oh, there were a few tricks. One of the requirements was that a cavalry horse had to be able to be ridden bareback 200 feet up to the British inspecting officer before he was examined. Some were pretty rank and it took a good rider to stay on. We'd station men with whips alongside the alley they had to ride up and it was the idea to get the horse to buck forward instead of up by hitting them with the whip when they started to buck. We didn't care if they bucked--as long as it was forward and the rider stayed on.

"If a horse or mule wasn't blind or lame or afflicted with heaves or stringhalt or any of a million other things a horse or mule can get, well, he passed, and the British branded a mark that looked like a crow's foot on his jaw or shoulder. After I got drafted and sent overseas when the United States entered the war and was in the Argonne, by God if some of the horses and mules we used didn't have that same crow's foot brand--they were Lathrop mounts.

"What I remember most is before I was drafted. Guyton & Harrington assembled the finest bunch of big sugar mules, all of them about 17 hands, and sent them over to London so the British could see just what fine animals we had to offer. And you know what happened. A German U-boat sent all 600 of them right to the bottom. Lord, they were fine mules."

After the war Van Buren returned to Lathrop, got married and became a farmer. He still owns about 900 acres in the area.

"It's just like when I talked to that Rotary Club group," he said. "You drive down the freeway now and look straight ahead, thinking only of today. But this land has seen more than just today. It's seen a lot of yesterdays, too."

School to Die with Pride Intact

BOGUE, Kan.--The class of '78 returned to the books here Tuesday, ending the last Christmas recess the high school will ever enjoy. It has run out of students.

The next months promise to be bittersweet for the 29 students of the old brick high school and for the residents of the town and the surrounding countryside.

Bogue High School, home of the Bluejays, is closing. Last month, patrons of the school voted 73-65 to close the school at the end of the spring term. Though some shop classes will be held in the 52-year-old structure next year, students will be bused nine miles west to Hill City High School, home of the Ringnecks.

"It's going to be a sad time when they lock the doors on the old place," says Leon Stephen, a school board member and alumnus of Bogue High. "There's a lot of memories there."

Memories notwithstanding, the board's recommendation to close the school was plain, hard-headed Kansas logic:

· The students weren't getting a high-quality education because of the low enrollment.

· Too many classes had only one student and there was a chance, because of the falling enrollment and the lack of courses, that Bogue would lose its accreditation by the Kansas Department of Education.

That reasoning was accepted. Despite the closeness of the vote, no one came up with a suggestion to try for one more year. In Bogue, the majority ruled.

But it wasn't an easy decision. Though the quality of the education brought the issue to a vote, there were other reasons.

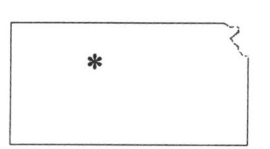

One, Stephen says, was that the board looked around the town and the surrounding area and didn't see many children who eventually would go to high school.

"It's not that the kids wouldn't enroll," he says. "It's that the kids just aren't there."

Bernard Allen, superintendent of Unified School District 281 in Hill City, puts it more graphically.

"Used to be when you went up to visit a friend in the hospital here you'd always stop by the maternity ward and see the babies," he says. "Not any more. Only once in a while do you see one. Maybe two at the most. But that's all.

"But then we're like every place else. There's a falling birthrate and that's a national trend. And then we're up here in northwest Kansas where population is declining. It's that simple. When I came up here in 1949, we had rural high schools at Webster, Prairie View, Densmore, Clayton and Bogue. And here in 1978 only Bogue is left. And it's going to close.

"What's happening is that we're running out of kids."

There was another reason, largely unspoken. The Lincoln Branch League removed Bogue from its 1978 football schedule, and there was talk of erasing Bogue from the Lincoln Branch 1978-79 basketball schedule. The reason: lack of players.

Football and basketball are big in Bogue.

"They bring the town together," says Doug Kysar, a shop teacher at the school.

But for fans and players, the 8-man football played here was a trial this year. In 1976 the Bluejays were the champions of all Kansas in 8-man football, the fast game played on an 80-by-40-yard field. It demands endurance and resilience, which means a squad needs more than eight players. Coach Dick Robinson ended up with fewer than that just before the Lucas-Luray game. He had seven players; three of them were freshmen.

Then a remarkable things happened. Two girls came out for the squad, juniors Tina Irby and Tammy Thompson. The story made the wire services across the country. There were a few quips about how Bogue played "8-person football."

Robinson played the girls, who weren't that much smaller than his male players. The heaviest squad member weighed 140 pounds. The coach said speed would overcome. Speed and one substitute player.

It didn't work. Lucas-Luray murdered Bogue, 46-14.

Tipton crushed Bogue, 50-14, and in the process Dan Irby broke his right ankle, leaving eight players on the squad.

Winona tri-Plains, with two starters weighing 230 and 285 pounds, walloped Bogue, 42-22. In that game, Ricky Johnson, described in the *Hill City Times* as "an outstanding 137-pound guard," dislocated his hip with two minutes left in the game. Bogue had only seven players left, so the game--along with the season--was called.

"I watched those kids," says Bob Boyd, an editor of the *Times*. "All of them, even the girls, played their hearts out. Good Lord, they were playing teams that outweighed them and out-numbered them. Those other teams were suiting up 25 to 30 players and running in defensive and offensive units. And our kids had to play the whole 60 minutes. Talk about courage. They never gave up."

That was it. The girls both had black eyes after the last game. Irby and Johnson were on crutches. There were other assorted aches, pains and bruises.

Bogue can be proud, even in defeat. The school produced college athletes, including Veryl Switzer, an All Big Eight back of the early 1950s at Kansas State University and a member of the National Football League's Green Bay Packers. Bogue finished the 1977 season amid a kind of splendid misery.

"We still thought they were winners," Stephen says.

The next months will have a flavor all their own for the students at Bogue. There undoubtedly will be thoughts of what could have been and what actually was. But next year the Bluejays will become Ringnecks at Hill City, playing 11- man football in the Mid-Continent League. For the girls there will be other sports, such as volleyball.

"The ironic thing about this, in a way," Allen says, "is that if we'd had volleyball at Bogue we probably couldn't have let the girls play. But the federal government said we couldn't discriminate under Title IX, so we didn't.

"How did I feel about it? Well, I was sick when the boys got hurt. And I was relieved when the girls didn't."

July 20, 1987

At Cow Paddy Nine, Golf's Fine

GRINNELL, Kan. -- Thank heaven it's Monday and the British Open is over.

Now there'll be some room on the sports pages for wrassling and more Bo Jackson stories and what pro football player got arrested for using his nose as a vacuum cleaner.

And for at least a week we'll be spared the sepulchral voices of the television commentators, whispering about the details of the Muirfield, Scotland, golf course, especially how difficult it gets when the wind and rain blow off something called the Firth of Forth, not to mention its deep bunkers and all the rest.

Now it's Monday and people here can get back to what counts--playing golf at the local links, "The Cow Paddy Nine."

Actually that name, while descriptive of the former use of the course's 37 acres, is purely a local term. The proper name for the nine holes just north of town and next to the Grinnell township cemetery is more formal-- "The Cow Paddy Club." There's a big sign attesting that fact right next to thedonated clubhouse, which is actually an old barn roof made into an A-frame that houses the lounge and maintenance shed.

Muirfield it ain't.

But there is a similarity on days when the wind here in western Kansas seems to blow hard enough to snap the links off a log chain. Out here, of course, wind like that is considered merely a gentle zephyr--nothing to get excited about, especially when you're busy lining up a putt or figuring out how to get over one of the two water hazards that are maybe 6 inches deep and lined with black plastic to keep the water in.

The Cow Paddy course is table-top flat, has limitless wheat and milo fields for scenery, and most likely will never see a Tom Watson or Lee Trevino tee off on the first hole.

But that's OK, because folks here are having a fine time. And to say they like their golf is an understatement. Grinnell has maybe 400 people in it. About 150 of them belong to the golf club--not a bad ratio, considering.

"We've got people here who never held a golf club until a couple of years ago," says Rick Tholen, a founder of the club. "Now you go out there and there's always people playing. There's three guys 80-plus, and they just seem to live out there."

So rabid for golf are Grinnell folks that a recent after-dark tournament, using balls that glow in the dark, was a smashing success.

The club was founded four years ago after Tholen, his brother Greg, Rick Wolf, Joe and Tom Beckman, Whitey Stuckoff, Mike Gallion and Don Felt were introduced to the game up in Oberlin. The course here on Ralph Hansen's pasture started out as four holes with 4-inch oil field well casing for cups and lengths of rod with socks tied to them for flagsticks. Tholen says the first year meant dodging cows and stepping over what cows leave behind. Finally, they got the pasture mowed, bought real cups and sticks, and planted rye grass for both the greens and fairways.

"The whole town pitched in," said Nita Huelsman, who keeps track of the $35 annual memberships ($25 for singles) and $3 green fees.

"Before golf?" Tholen reflected. "Well, people used to go over to Oakley and drive around. Or have a few beers. Now it seems everybody plays golf."

No, Tholen added, there aren't any plans for a pro shop.

"Most people get their clubs from Wal-Mart," he said. "We're not that fancy yet, but you know, the Co-op gas station is selling golf balls now."

November 14, 1990

Tale of Two Bills Points Up Truman's Honesty

(KANSAS CITY, Mo.)--The papers say Harry S. Truman's presidential yacht, the *Williamsburg*, is in awful shape resting near a Potomac river sewage plant outside Washington.

Trees are growing through the deck, trash litters the deck, parts of the vessel are simply rotting, and vandals have done their work.

Seven million dollars to even start to fix it up, say the folks who should know. And if nothing happens, get ready for the steel hull to be cut up for scrap in 1992.

The *Williamsburg*. For those old enough, even the mention of the yacht instantly conjures up that bespectacled little fellow whose morning walks left reporters wheezing, who said what he thought, and came from Independence.

The *Williamsburg*? Well, that's where Truman played a lot of poker--a good Missouri card game and one that drove a lot of Republicans and others who thought they had a lock on public morals absolutely bonkers.

What's been forgotten--but what the *Williamsburg* refocuses--is the dislike a lot of people had for Truman back in the late 1940s. He didn't look presidential. There was no way he could be mistaken for that patrician named Franklin D. Roosevelt who'd preceded him in office. Playing poker on the Williamsburg, said his critics, hinted what sort of man he was.

Well, not exactly.

Listen to Yancey Wasson, who lives in Truman's hometown. He's got a yarn about Truman that sort of flies in the face of those long-ago innuendos and persnickety comments.

Yancey's 81. He's had a lot of jobs--hardware salesman, engineer, writer. That last is his avocation now. Between Thanksgiving and Dec. 1 another of his books will be out. *Early Times in Lineville, Vol II* is mainly stories about southern Iowa and northern Missouri, but it has a couple of tales from Yancey's years in Kansas City thrown in.

In the book is Yancey's Truman story. It goes like this:

Back in 1933 Yancey was working at Guy Wasson's Fabric Co., at 2920 McGee Trafficway in Kansas City. Guy was his cousin, and Yancey, since the Depression was a grinding fact of life, was happy to have a job. The pay was $12 a week. Yancey not only sold seat covers for cars, he installed them.

Well, one day Harry S. Truman, presiding judge of the Jackson County court, walked in. Truman wanted a nice herringbone pattern, medium brown in color, for his Chrysler.

The deal was made and Truman left the car with Yancey. By evening he had the car finished and delivered it to Truman. The bill was $32.

"My cousin, Guy, told me to tell Mr. Truman that if he could give us some business on county cars and trucks, he could forget about the bill," says Yancey.

That's how things were done. One hand washed the other.

Well, Yancey made his pitch and what he got from Truman was a look. One look.

"Son, I don't do business that way," said Truman. Then he wrote Yancey a check for $32, which back then was considerable money.

The rest of the story happened a few weeks later. Tom Pendergast, then political boss of Kansas City, Jackson County and most of Missouri as well, got seat covers for his Cadillac sedan. Pendergast's bill was $65, pocket change for him.

Yancey delivered the car. And as he had with Truman, he gave his pitch: forget the bill if you can throw some business our way.

"Tom leaned back in his big chair behind his even bigger desk," recalls Yancey, "cleared his throat and said, 'I think we can do that.'"

Pendergast gave Yancey a card and wrote the name of the manager of the Kansas City police garage on it. See this man, he told Yancey, who stuck Pendergast's unpaid bill in his pocket.

"About two hours later," Yancey says, "I walked out of the police garage with an order for 200 quick-change seat covers for 100 cars on the police register and an order for 20 front rubber mats."

And that's Yancey's story. Two men. Two bills. One paid, the other not.

"If you'd asked me which one would have been president that day, I would have said Pendergast," Yancey says. "No two ways about it."

December 1, 1983

Mayor Is a One-man Dynasty

WEIR, Kan. -- The mayor, namely Billy Gowans, age 83, was in. As usual, he was sucking on his pipe. As usual, he was wearing his yellow cap.

Over to the left of Mr. Gowans was Mitch Van Camp, 19, the city clerk, who just then was being forcefully reminded by Mr. Gowans, a great baseball fan, that he--Mr. Van Camp--had once hit 28 home runs playing Little League baseball. Mr. Gowans was Mr. Van Camp's coach then. Mr. Van Camp, on the telephone, nodded.

In front of Mr. Gowans was his daughter, Ann Gowans, the assistant city clerk. Miss Gowans was working on the books. Her father watched.

As mayor of Weir, Mr. Gowans makes $5 a month, which is a darned sight more than he used to make when custom called for the $1-a-year salary to be turned back to the city.

"Now I'm in the big money," said the mayor, reveling in the thought of a whole five bucks a month.

Billy Gowans, in reality, would do his job for a lot less.

Still, the pressures of his office are getting to him. He doesn't know whether he'll run come 1985, when his current term expires. He had similar doubts in last spring's city election.

Mr. Gowans waited until five minutes before the filing deadline, saw that no one else was about to file, sighed, and threw his hat into the ring.

"Oh, people call me up all the time and give me hell," he said. "You know, over the $75 we charge for water meter deposits now. But we had to. People were coming in in trailers, hooking up and then leaving without paying their bills."

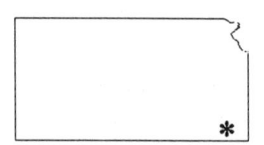

Mr. Gowans -- who has been a coal miner, construction worker and Highway Department employee and now is the man who carries the flowers from the local funeral home to the grave site -- was asked about his hearing. It might help to be a little hard of hearing when people call late. But Mr. Gowans allowed that his hearing was good.

"Fair," said his daughter, under her breath.

Well, maybe fair, said Mr. Gowans.

"I've got the ability to let it in one ear and out the other," he said, grinning.

Mr. Gowans also has remarkable endurance. He's been mayor of this small Cherokee County town since 1931 -- 52 years. To put that in perspective, Herbert Hoover was president when Mr. Gowans took office; John F. Kennedy was 14 years old; and Chick Hafey of the Cardinals won the National League batting title by the slimmest of margins.

Until the Royals, Mr. Gowans was a big Cardinal fan. He is always devoted to playing pitch and bingo. Mr. Gowans loves bingo.

As far as he knows, Mr. Gowans is the oldest continuously elected official in the state.

"I got an award on my 48th year over in Wichita," he said. "When I was there some guy from Hugoton was working on 40 years. I was that far ahead."

Mr. Gowans was sitting behind a table in the Victorian City Hall here, built in 1882. A small piece of marble, shaped like a grave marker, was in front of him with his name spelled out. A tombstone cutter gave him the sign as a present Mr. Gowans, who has arresting blue eyes, said he was in good health, adding that you have to be in his job.

Mr. Gowans can remember only one opponent in all those years, despite the fact that he's a rock-ribbed Republican in a town where being a Democrat is as common as breathing. Years ago a woman mounted a challenge. Mr. Gowans beat her by a 4-1 margin. In this year's election, he ran unopposed. As usual, he didn't campaign. In fact, he's never given a political speech. He got 141 of the 156 votes cast.

"The 15 votes I didn't get were people who either forgot or didn't like me and that's how they let me know," he said.

In this job, he went on, you don't always make friends.

Still, over the years, Mr. Gowans, a Weir native and avid booster, has made a lot of friends. The ball fields here are named after him, since not only has he been a fan but he played until he was in his 50s, not really that long ago.

Weir, Mr. Gowans said, is on the move with new housing, a larger tax base, and a new sewer system. Those are big things in a small town, he added. But he does wish the sales tax had passed in the last election.

"A lady called me up after and complained about a pothole in front of her driveway," he said. "Asked when the city would fix it. Well, she'd fought the sales tax.

"I said to her, 'You got any friends?' 'Why?' she says. 'Because,' I said, 'without that sales tax money you'll have to fix it yourself.'

"Well, made her think. But you know, that's what you got to do. Too many people in government talk out of the side of their mouth."

That's Billy Gowans. Fifty-two years of service. And plain talk.

CCC Camp Shelters Memories

BRADLEYVILLE, Mo. -- There were about 100 of them, all in their 60s and 70s now, the men wearing sport shirts and the women wearing dresses, picking their way along a graveled road, staying away from the weeds and the chiggers and the tiny seed ticks.

For most of the women, it was all new. For the men it was a return to a part of their lives that once seemed so big they swore they'd never forget. But they had. What had seemed so familiar 40 years ago no longer was familiar at all. Oh, bits and pieces were there but not the full tapestry of what they recollected. The marching, camaraderie, and hard work, and the simple knowledge that they were making their way had been swallowed by time and the pines and the scrub oak that have engulfed the land.

"That's where the gas pumps and oil was kept," said one man, looking at some concrete amid the brush. "But I don't remember it exactly there. And I remember it bigger, lots bigger."

The boys of Company No. 1733, Civilian Conservation Corps, the New Deal program that put almost 3 million young men to work in the mid-1930s and early 1940s, came home to their old camp in the Mark Twain National Forest south of here last weekend, their wives and memories in tow.

They had taken a bus or driven their cars to a point two miles south of here and then turned east along a trace the Ava district of the U.S. Forest Service had bladed out. At a point just west of where the old water tower sat--only the footings remain--the bus and cars had parked. There was another quarter of a mile walk to the concrete slab where the motor pool sat. Above there, fanned out, had been the barracks, parade grounds, mess hall, even a goldfish pond-- all the support facilities the corps needed to keep 190 men in the woods planting trees, building roads, cutting brush, and building fire towers.

All the buildings are gone now, rooted out in the first days of World War II and moved God only knows where. But the area remains "the old CCC camp," says Jerry Decker, a ranger. He put together old pictures of the camp and copies of the camp newspaper, *The Ridge Runner,* in a scrapbook and laid it out on the hood of his pickup. The men gathered around the truck and tried to identify who was in the old Kodaks, as they were called then, and read the names in the paper, recalling some who'd died in the war, others who couldn't be at the reunion, and several who had died of plain old age.

Looking at the scrapbook, the men became animated, remembering the years the camp was open, between 1939 and 1942, refreshing each other's memories about a fist fight or a particularly raucous trip to town. Away from the men, their wives visited, waiting for a picnic lunch to begin.

Earnest Rodgers of Springfield, Mo., who had been the supply clerk at the camp--he couldn't get work as a schoolteacher--said that there were a few bad apples in the corps, just like in any group, but that by and large the ones who had survived the war became upright, decent citizens, paying taxes, marrying, rearing families and always looking back on their years in the corps with a deep and shining pride.

"I think, like me, they found being in the CCC meant they learned they could always get a hand to help them," said Mr. Rodgers, who fought his way across the Pacific Ocean. And with that Mr. Rodgers made his point, grasping the wrist of his right hand with the fingers of his left.

Ralph Wilson, who became a successful California building contractor, remembered the corps as an adventure and laughed that one of his memories was of coming to camp having heard of Jell-O but never having seen it.

"We couldn't afford Jell-O," he said.

Lee Cooley grew up on 40 acres near Drury, with seven brothers and sisters.

"We had six acres of bottom land in corn, said Mr. Cooley, a retired poultry farmer. "My father would work for a day at a time for a man, and that man would pay him in molasses. Our cows were dried up from the drought, and the government took them, giving Daddy $13, I think, for all of them. And that one winter before I came to the CCC we lived on corn, molasses and cowpeas. That was all we had.

"So I came. Thirty dollars a month seemed like all the money in the world. I got to keep $5, and the government sent my mother and daddy the other $25.. And that's how my family made it through the Depression, on my pay.

"Poor? Oh sure we were poor, 'ceptin' we really didn't know it. You know what this was for most of us? Simple. It was opportunity."

June 1, 1982

Museum Could Use a Few 'Ahs'

CHANUTE, Kan.-- This being Kansas, Sondra Alden facetiously figures that what she ought to do to attract visitors to the museum she directs here is paint the bricks out in front yellow in honor of Dorothy and the Wizard of Oz, have a daily shoot-out rivaling the one in Dodge City, get a ball of twine to rival Cawker City's and contract for a hand-dug well like the one at Greensburg.

Mrs. Alden and Barbara Henshall, respectively the director and volunteer curator of the Martin and Osa Johnson Safari Museum, are frustrated.

"Here we've got a unique museum, one where scholar and layman alike can see something they can see nowhere else in the world, and we're ignored," Mrs. Alden said. "Sometimes, I want to weep."

The latest blow came last month when a Kansas newspaper extolled Kansas vacations, listing such attractions as Dodge City, the Greyhound Hall of Fame and the Eisenhower Library in Abilene, the Chalk pyramids, and touting the "Kansas, Land of Ahs" theme that's being promoted by Kansas' travel and tourism division.

Mrs. Alden said, "I think if I hear 'Land of Ahs' any more, I'll throw up."

What cut the two women was that the article didn't mention the Safari Museum. Nor was the museum mentioned in an earlier tourism division press release about places to go and things to do in Kansas. "If it isn't Dorothy and the yellow brick road or Matt Dillon, forget it," Mrs. Alden said.

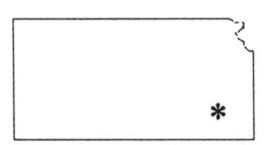

Mrs. Henshall, who does public relations for the museum, sent off a smoking letter to the newspaper. The letter, in part, read:

"As usually, there was no mention of the museum (in the tourism division's press release). I know. . .Topeka knows about us, but they never seem to remember us when the time comes to give out information about places to visit in Kansas. I will grant we are not on I-35 or I-70 but we do have highways that pass through or near Chanute.

"While it may seem strange to have a museum without displays of barbed wire, we do have a saddle. Unfortunately it is for a camel....Instead of (photographs of) early settlers, we present photographs of early travels to the South Seas, Africa, and Borneo. There isn't much to say about the attire of the people in the pictures, for some aren't attired at all.

"Our primitive art is not by itinerant painters but by the blacksmiths of West Africa. We do not have trophies of deer but of antelope and gazelle. Our buffalo are Cape buffalos."

Mrs. Alden said nobody from the tourism division has even bothered to visit the museum, which will celebrate its 21st anniversary next month. That seems strange, she said, since Martin Johnson was from Independence, Kan., and his wife, Osa Leighty Johnson, was from Chanute. Osa, incidentally, was sort of the Bo Derek of her day, a pretty-full-figured woman who drew lines to movie houses in the 1920s and 1930s when six Johnson full-length movies, numerous one-reelers, and books made the couple's name a household word.

Martin died in a plane crash in 1937. Osa continued to write, lecture, and travel until her death in the early 1950s. After that, the thousands of artifacts, photographs, carvings, films and other tons of items the Johnsons brought home from what they called their "adventures" gathered dust in the attic of Belle Leighty, Osa's mother, until they went to the museum in 1961.

In the years since, the private museum and its 5,000 book library, one of five in Kansas recognized by the American Association of Museums, has existed on small admission charges and donations. There's no public relations budget, Mrs. Henshall said.

Being ignored by the state has hurt, Mrs. Alden said. Attendance last year was down to about 10,000 visitors. But surprisingly, calls and visitors still come from the British Broadcasting Company, the National Geographic Society, and scholarly institutions all over the world. "I didn't even know you existed," said one recent visitor to the museum, which is just west of downtown.

Mrs. Alden said: "I'm sure Kenya or New York would be delighted to have this museum and collection, if for no other reason than it's a repository of evidence about the ecological changes that have taken place in Africa and the South Pacific in the last 50 years. But really, all we're asking is just a little notice from Kansas."

October 17, 1981

Folks All Said Ralph Was Nuts

STOCKTON, Mo.--Back then--the fall and winter of 1945--everybody thought Ralph Hammons had lost his mind.

They included the bankers who were lending him money to buy 3 million pounds of what most people figured was a stinking nuisance.

They wondered why. Ralph had a good business here. In his grocery just off the Stockton square you could buy groceries and sell your rabbits, feed, eggs, and just about anything else produced on farms. A buying station was what people called such stores.

But then they knew Ralph. He worked hard. Too hard, some said. The man couldn't sit still. Had to have something to do. And now this--3 millions pounds of walnuts.

He was even paying people a few cents a pound to bring those awful, moldy old things that fell off the walnut trees into his store in sacks. Then he was throwing the sacks on railroad cars for shipment to a Virginia processing plant.

By the spring of 1946 everybody was sure Ralph had learned his lesson. The freight to Virginia was a steep price to pay. But Ralph, then in his early 30s, still had a glint in his eye. By summer workmen were building machinery on a lot just north of town. Processing, Ralph told anyone who would listen, would be done right here in Stockton.

Hell, boys, he'd say, these walnuts are a crop just like hay or grain or hogs. There's money here. We've sat for years and squashed them underfoot. Maybe a few people have gotten out a hammer or a big rock and smashed up a few for their own use, but we've been wasting a resource.

That year Ralph Hammons processed 100,000 pounds of walnuts. That's down from 3 million but the freight was cheaper. And that, said Dwain Hammons, son of the late Ralph Hammons, is how it all started.

Mr. Hammons, a dark-haired man of 47 with a friendly smile, leaned back and thought about his father--part genius, part visionary, a pragmatist who coupled hard-headed business sense with the nerve of a Mississippi River gambler.

And most of all, Ralph Hammons was a hard worker. He died in 1973 from heart failure, but really from overworking. His health broke in the 1950s. Dwain Hammons came back from the service to take over the company in 1956. Still Ralph Hammons often came to the office. When he died at 59, Hammons Products was the world's largest walnut processor. Today the family-owned business is even bigger, with another processing plant in Bolivar, Mo. Hammons will process 30 million pounds of nuts this year.

"Quite simply," Mr. Hammons said, "the demand is always ahead of the supply."

That statement, the dream of any entrepreneur, bothers Mr. Hammons. He figures 50 percent of the walnut crop rots on the ground every year in the green, pulpy hulls that eventually blacken from the tannic acid they contain.

Mr. Hammons wants those walnuts and has established 196 buying stations in Missouri and Kansas to get them.

"You can figure that the average walnut, lying on the ground, is worth half a cent," he said. "That's a rough estimate."

Glenn Edmonds, Hammons' marketing director, put it more simply: "People will walk up and down a highway looking in the grass for aluminum beer cans worth a penny each. With walnuts, just find a tree. You can be pretty sure there'll be walnuts under it."

"Our job," Mr. Hammons added, "has been to educate farmers, landowners and the public that there's cash laying around out there. Right now we're paying 8 cents a pound, hulled, for nuts. That's $50 to $60 a pick-up load. That's money.

"We can buy that high because we not only use the nutmeat but because the shells have become valuable as metal abrasives, explosive additives, stuff they put in women's face-cleansing creams, and a material the oil companies use to seal the wells while they're drilling."

The big money is still in the extracted nutmeat. Although some meat is shipped to fill gift orders from a catalog that Hammons published, most leaves on tractor-trailers packed with 35-pound boxes destined for bakeries, ice cream factories, and candy plants. Each load is insured for $140,000, the value of the walnuts, which sell for $4.40 a pound.

Not bad. Especially since everybody knew as far back as 1945 that Ralph Hammons had lost his mind when he decided to sell something nobody else wanted.

October 21, 1990

Kansas and Missouri Melted into One for Early Miners

BURGESS, Mo.--This town got its name in the 1880s from a Kentuckian named--what else--Burgess, who got interested in the coal mining possibilities hereabouts.

Old Burgess--his first name has been lost--was no dummy. There was coal here, lots of it. A hundred years ago this part of Barton County and Crawford County, Kan., just across the state line, teemed with people, most of them foreign-born. They dug coal, first in deep shaft mines whence they hauled it out by the bushel, and then by using huge shovels that stripped the coal from beneath the land, leaving long pits and high tailings.

Every crossroads had a mine. There was Burgess and neighboring Mulberry, Fuller and Curranville, Foxton and Red Onion.

The English language? Well, occasionally. The story goes that 80 years ago you could stand in downtown Pittsburg, Kan., the nearest big town, and hear 20 foreign languages, maybe more.

Burgess, always in the shadow of Mulberry, was full of Austrians and Italians. And, of course, the Dubrays and the Marchands who spoke French. They knew coal, being from that part of France near the Belgian border.

There was a Burgess school, grades one through eight. Back 30-40 years ago, a kid getting out of school had a choice of high schools: Mindenmines and Liberal in Missouri or the Mulberry high school over in Kansas. A lot of Missouri kids west to Mulberry. No big deal. They just went.

Eventually, Mulberry got to be a fair-sized town of maybe 600 people; Burgess, just across the road, had Panizzi's Grocery, long-since closed, and a dance hall, which is now used for storage.

And there was the one other thing that made Burgess different--a liquor store sitting right there on the state line across from "dry" Kansas.

The Dubrays ran it, first Madeline, and then her daughter Minnie, now 83 and in bad shape up at the hospital in Fort Scott, Kan. She broke her arm, couldn't handle the walker, then fell and broke her hip, says her son, Tony Dubray Jr.

"I don't think she has a lot of time," Tony says.

"Oh, but she's something. She opened up when she got up and closed down when she went to bed. Busy? You bet. Look where she was."

Last week Tony was in the store, waiting for the occasional customer to wander through the door. He's still re-ordering beer, cigarettes, pop and chips. He's cut back the hours of the store from 4 to 7 p.m.

And he's selling out the liquor and wine. When the hard stuff is gone, he'll probably offer the store for sale. He doubts that he'll be able to sell it, although he allows a guy could make a living if he'd turn it into a convenience store.

"We're all that's left in Burgess," he says.

Tony's 60. He was a high school principal in Liberal for years and years. It just about kills him to see what has happened to Mulberry and Burgess, towns that spawned hard-working people from what essentially was a goulash of nationalities.

They were people who mostly got along with one another. Who loved and laughed, played baseball with abandon (at one time there were eight town teams in Mulberry and Burgess), loved their basketball teams and were fiercely proud of being where they were from.

And where was that? Missouri? Kansas? Who cared about that?

They were from where the tailing stood and people dug coal. They were from that area between U.S. 69 and 71 where a lot of the land now looks like a moonscape and where differences in philosophical outlook, likely as not, were settled with a punch in the snoot.

It was tough country. But good people.

And now one more of its landmarks, Dubray's Place, is getting ready to fade away.

Over in Mulberry, there's just a service station and a weekly newspaper. And the post office that serves both towns.

"I know one place that won't miss us a bit," Tony says when he considers closing Dubray's. "Jefferson City. You know why? Because it's always driven them crazy having to mail a Missouri liquor license to Kansas."

January 11, 1988

For Want of a Vote, He Lost It

TOPEKA -- Politics used to be a lot less complicated. Witness Gary Hart and his love life or Sen. Joe Biden and his misstatements.

Now comes Sen. Bob Dole and a little question of some forgeries on his Texas nominating petitions.

Wouldn't it be simpler if all that stood in the way of a candidate being nominated or not came down to a buffalo hunter getting lost in a snowstorm?

Well, that's exactly what happened in Kansas.

The candidate in this case was the wonderfully named Marcus Junius Parrott, handsome, imperious, and as contemporary accounts said, "a born orator, a delight the moment he stepped onto a stage."

Parrott was seen as a comer. He was a South Carolinian by birth but hated slavery. After a few years in Ohio (and two terms in the state legislature), he arrived in Kansas in 1855. In 1857 he was elected as the territorial delegate to the U.S. Congress.

In 1861, Kansas became a state. And Marcus Junius Parrott wanted more than anything to be a U.S. senator. Somehow, that lust seems familiar in this political year of 1988.

And Parrott had a chance. Everybody knew crazy Jim Lane would be one of the two senators. Parrott was the odds-on favorite for the other seat.

The man, however, had enemies. He was too glib, they said. Not sincere. The meanest jab came from one man who wrote: "Parrott should have been a Parisian." Those were harsh words in Kansas.

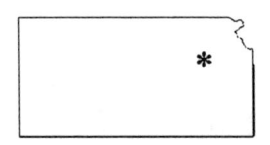

Enter one Ernest Hohneck who would play a fateful role in Parrott's political future. The two men, according to Hohneck, were not acquainted. They should have been because of the rather amazing parallels in their lives.

Like Parrott, Hohneck, a native of Germany, was born in the fall of 1828. He emigrated to the United States, resided briefly in New York, and then continued on to Cincinnati. His success in Ohio was considerably less than Parrott's, understandable since Hohneck's trade was newspapering.

In 1855, the same year as Parrott, Hohneck came to Kansas, settling in Wabaunsee County. And in 1857, while Parrott went off to Washington, Hohneck was elected to the first territorial legislature.

By 1861, Hohneck was an avid Parrott man. The (Republican) legislature would nominate--and then, as was the custom--elect. Nomination, therefore, was tantamount to election.

But voting for Parrott wasn't the only thing on Hohneck's mind.

There was a little matter of eating.

"If all of Wabaunsee County had been stood on its head," Hohneck remembered, "I doubt if $100 could have been shaken out of their pockets."

Hohneck resolved to go buffalo hunting so he could at least put some meat on the table. He would be back in time for the voting.

Well, he wasn't. A snowstorm on the western Kansas plains marooned Hohneck near Ness City for several weeks. He was reported dead.

Guess what? The politicians got together and Parrott missed being nominated for the U.S. Senate by a single vote. Parrott would try again in 1862 and 1874. And fail. He died a penniless and broken man a few years later.

Hohneck left Kansas in 1883 and settled in Spokane, Wash. Queried in 1908 about his legislative days, Hohneck said he'd been trying to forget that buffalo hunt and the missed vote for 47 years and hoped everybody else had forgotten it too.

Which kind of shows how politics has changed in 127 years. Today Hohneck would write an instant book, then get an agent and go on all the talk shows.

May 10, 1991

Before the Ax, Raytown Trees Were Living History

(KANSAS CITY, Mo.)--Raytown South High School looms across the street from 83rd and Sterling in Raytown. It's a monolith of brick and glass that blocks the view of what old-timers hereabouts still refer to as Old 50 Highway.

The high school was built on what was the old Fetter place. In fact, 83rd Street used to be called Fetter Road, named after the family who farmed the land and lived in the old brick house that had been built in 1850.

Legend has it that during the Civil War the Fetter place was William Clarke Quantrill's headquarters. There he planned his bloody raids on the blue-bellied Kansans, plotted against Jennison's Jayhawkers, succored his wounded.

Legend also has it that "secesh" casualties were tended in an upstairs room, one that subsequent generations of Fetters scrubbed and cleaned. But to no avail--the pooled bloodstains on the floor were permanent.

The house and farm land eventually fell to what's called progress. Bulldozers came in and cleared the high school site, covering what some claimed was a treasure, the ill-gotten swag from Quantrill's raids that had been buried somewhere on the farm.

Still, there was one reminder of the old days--a line of cedar trees extending along the south side of 83rd Street.

The cedars were right across the road from the Fetter place on what was known as the Gault farm.

This part of Jackson County was still country when the trees were planted in the 1880s. It was a good day's trip by wagon or buggy to Kansas City and back.

The cedars were set out by the family of George N. Gault, who bought and cleared the hilly land after the war. The reason was probably twofold--to mark his north boundary line and to provide some beauty in what must have been a life full of hard, thankless work.

The trees were planted every 20 or so feet and left to grow. In time they became magnificent trees, the lower branches falling away, the trunks thickening, the boughs ever green.

A century passed. In that time some trees fell to disease. Others were cut down as the land went from farm to subdivision.

But a few remained--the four on the southeast corner of 83rd and Sterling, one about a quarter-mile to the east, another just to the west of Sterling in Byron Kenshow's front yard.

"The four trees on the corner was where high school kids went," Jerry Justice said. "You know kids. They'd stand there off school property, shoot the bull, act cool and smoke. Under the trees."

The cedars were more than just a hangout. Justice used them for directions.

"Turn at the trees," he'd tell people coming to his house in the 8400 block of Sterling. "You can't miss them."

So imagine Justice's surprise last week when he came home from work, got ready to make his turn on Sterling and looked for the big trees.

They were gone.

"Cut down," Justice said. "All that was left was trunks and branches (on the ground). Just like that."

Dennis Henry, assistant director of public works for Raytown, said the trees were cut down to make room for the installation of curbing on 83rd Street. He said he'd heard of no protests about their removal.

"Protest?" Justice said. "One day they were there, the next day they were gone."

What gripes Justice is that the cedars were landmarks. They were history. Maybe they weren't as fancy as that fountain in the silk-stocking section of Kansas City that's now filling up most of the letters-to-the-editor section of the newspaper.

But to some folks here those old trees were friends, something that was a regular as the spring rain.

They were planted by real people who knew that with some tending they'd grow and provide shade and define their piece of the world.

Meyer Circle? Face it. Old J.C. Nichols bought some cheap, unwanted statuary in Italy, stuck it out in some pasture land he was trying to peddle and called it "art." Which is what's getting all the ink. Not four trees in Raytown.

"I know," Justice said. "They were just trees. I guess we'll get used to it. But I can't drive by without seeing them. And it makes me sick."

December 30, 1987

Paper Had Lead Type and Iron Men

LECOMPTON, Kan. -- You can see it coming.

Gary Hart's ahead in the polls, and some are jumping aboard his bandwagon. After all, everybody just knows the so-called media are to blame for asking Hart those nasty questions last May.

You can bet some political columnists soon will be saying that Gary Hart, while maybe a little randy, isn't half bad, that he's admitted his mistakes, that maybe he is "electable."

It used to be simpler. Wishy-washy wasn't in the press's vocabulary.

Why down at Lamar, Mo., old Arthur Aull would write in the *Lamar Democrat* who'd been found dead drunk on the courthouse lawn. What husband had been sleeping around. And with whom. Or which daughter of a leading family was expecting.

Aull would name names, dates, places, etc. A spade was a spade. Of course Aull wasn't part of the "media" then. He was just a cantankerous old newspaperman who put in print what everybody was talking about anyway.

Ditto what happened here 131 years ago. In those days, the press didn't fool around.

The background was this:

The abolitionists who'd settled over east at Lawrence in the mid-1850s had started a newspaper called *The Herald of Freedom*. Abolitionist and newspaperman meant roughly the same thing then. The sheet didn't take kindly to the pro-slavery folks over in Missouri and said so. The Missourians reciprocated and, tiring of what they perceived as the paper's overly critical comments, came to Lawrence, ransacked the newspaper's office, smashed the press, and then dumped the whole thing in the Kansas River.

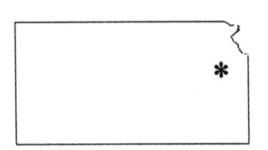

Part of the press and several thousand pounds of lead type, however, were recovered.

One of the Missourians' strongholds at the time was a reinforced cabin near Lecompton. It had the rather imposing name of Fort Titus. And it was a thorn in the side of the free-state men.

Still, the abolitionists had an ace up their sleeves. Well, not an ace. More like a cannon, one called "Old Sacramento."

What better retaliation for the newspaper raid, the free-staters thought, than "Old Sacramento" blowing Fort Titus to kingdom come?

Harsh, you say. But then people back in 1856 were a little more direct than they are today. Revenge wasn't a dirty word.

Alas, the free-staters had no cannon balls. But they did have a lot of lead type that had been pulled out of the river. And they had an expert machinist who whittled a wooden mold to make the cannon balls.

Eventually, 100 balls were cast, "Old Sacramento" was trained on Fort Titus, powder was loaded, a ball was inserted and a match applied.

The gun roared. And several free-staters/newspapermen yelled:

"*The Herald of Freedom* is issued again."

That was a nice touch. And Fort Titus, not surprisingly, was reduced to kindling in a matter of minutes.

Naturally, that couldn't happen now. Newspapers are produced now with computers. Lead has gone the way of the dodo bird. What prints many papers now is a plastic or aluminum mat attached to a press.

Which in a way says something about the way the whole country has gone in almost a century and a half.

Plastic candidates. Plastic mats.

And neither one worth loading into "Old Sacramento" to blow Fort Titus to smithereens. In fact, if Fort Titus were still standing, there probably wouldn't be a bunch of armed wild-eyed Missourians inside. There'd just be a bunch of people Xeroxing "position papers."

February 28, 1990

More Than a Name: A Friend

(KANSAS CITY, Mo.)--Jesse and Frank James? Eugene Field? Ernest Hemingway? That's a set of disparate names. But there's a legacy concerning all of them in the old brick building at 18th and Grand where for most of its existence, a newspaper called *The Kansas City Times* has been published.

History? Well, it was the voice of the "Lost Cause of the Confederacy," catering to those unreconstructed rebels who refused to forget the Civil War or their hatred for the blue-bellied Yankees. To this newspaper, the Jameses and Youngers, local boys, were heroes.

The Times was home to Eugene Field, who wrote wonderful children's poetry. Wynken, Blynken and Nod? That was Field.

Hemingway? He was in here before he went off to World War I. He claimed Pete Wellington, the *Times'* night editor, taught him how to write. High praise, indeed.

Still, there comes a moment when history just stops. Like today. Sometime this evening the first copies of Kansas City's new morning paper, *The Star*, will start rolling off the presses.

And *The Times* will simply disappear.

How quick? Well, this week the pasted-on names saying *Times* on the delivery trucks will be coated with a special solution that dissolves their adhesive backing. Some of the dispatch delivery cars had their signs removed last week.

That quick.

The reason is simple. Afternoon papers don't cut it anymore. Two hundred and seventy-nine have died since 1946. Only 10 or so afternoon papers remain in major markets. Just last fall the *Los Angeles Herald-Examiner* went belly up.

So the afternoon paper, *The Star*, is dying. Yet in death, it will live as the new morning *Star*, and *The Times* will fade away.

Unlike the *Herald-Examiner*, the end of *The Times* isn't exactly a classic newspaper death, one that brings anguished screams and post-mortems from editorial writers on other sheets, sad pictures of reporters and editors cleaning out their desks, condolences from civic leaders.

And yawns from the public who'd rather turn on the tube in the evening than read a newspaper.

But it is hard. The name of a newspaper--my newspaper for 30 years and the one my father worked on before me--won't be around anymore.

Plans are to put a plaque on a side of the building. People put up plaques for all sorts of lesser things these days. It'll say that in this city a pretty fair newspaper was published for over a century.

Yet no plaque can compensate for the memories--of old typewriters and linotype machines; the niggardly pay; the scowling editors; the ink and noise from the rumbling presses that literally shook the building when they roared to life; and, above all, the parade of characters who inhabited the *Times'* newsroom.

Now it's all computers and video display terminals, laser printers and fax machines. And the people who, since Watergate, have swarmed over what's now called the newspaper "profession," a fancy word for what is really no more than a craft. And some of those people seem to have the mission of writing about things, not people.

Yet the real pain is that the end of a familiar name will neatly bracket my own youth and early middle age.

Now, inexorably, will come the subtle deadening of memories, some funny, some bittersweet.

A plaque on a brick wall on a downtown street. It seems hardly enough for a paper called *The Times* that for all those years meant that morning had arrived in a goodly part of Missouri and Kansas. And that underneath that wonderful Gothic script was at least one story that fulfilled the daily dream of any reporter and editor--or that made a reader say, "Well, I'll be damned."

--30--